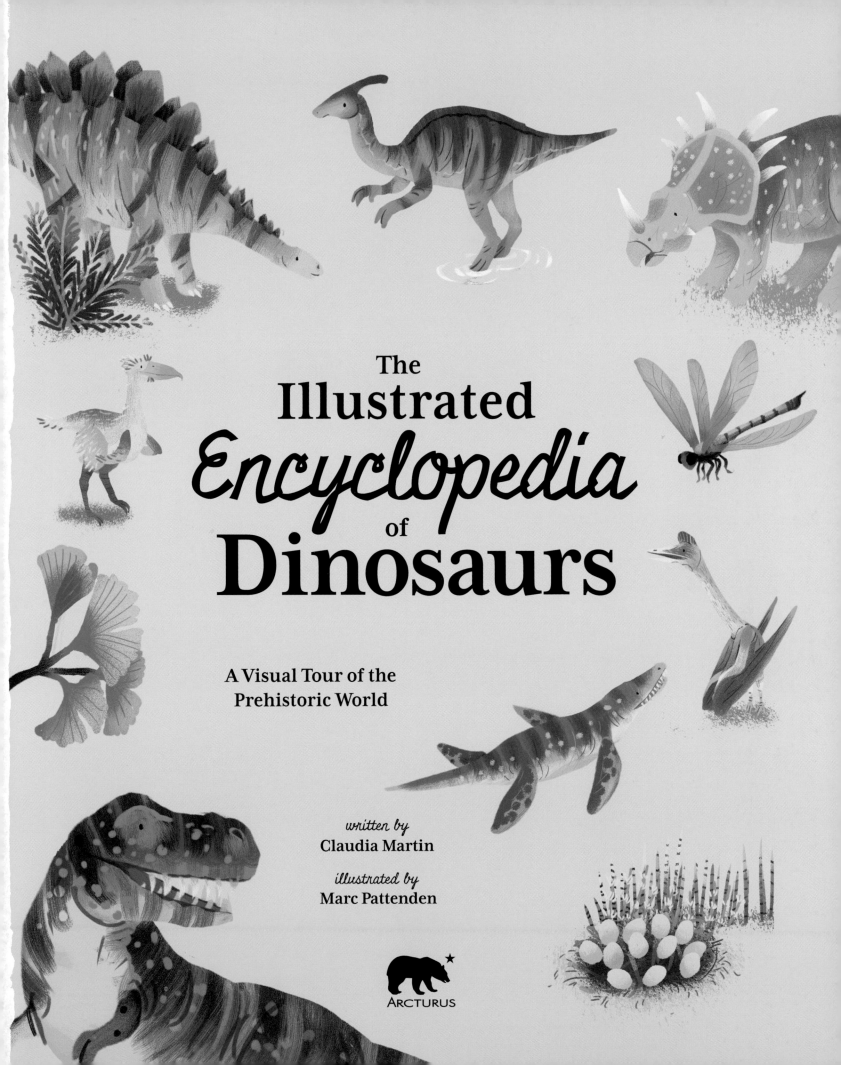

The
Illustrated
Encyclopedia
of
Dinosaurs

**A Visual Tour of the
Prehistoric World**

written by
Claudia Martin

illustrated by
Marc Pattenden

ARCTURUS

ARCTURUS

This edition published in 2023 by Arcturus Publishing Limited
26/27 Bickels Yard, 151–153 Bermondsey Street,
London SE1 3HA

Author: Claudia Martin
Illustrator: Marc Pattenden
Designer: Suzanne Cooper
Consultant: Dougal Dixon
Editor: Becca Clunes
Design manager: Jessica Holliland
Managing editor: Joe Harris

ISBN: 978-1-3988-3123-0
CH010464NT
Supplier 29, Date 0623, PI 00003557

Printed in China

Contents

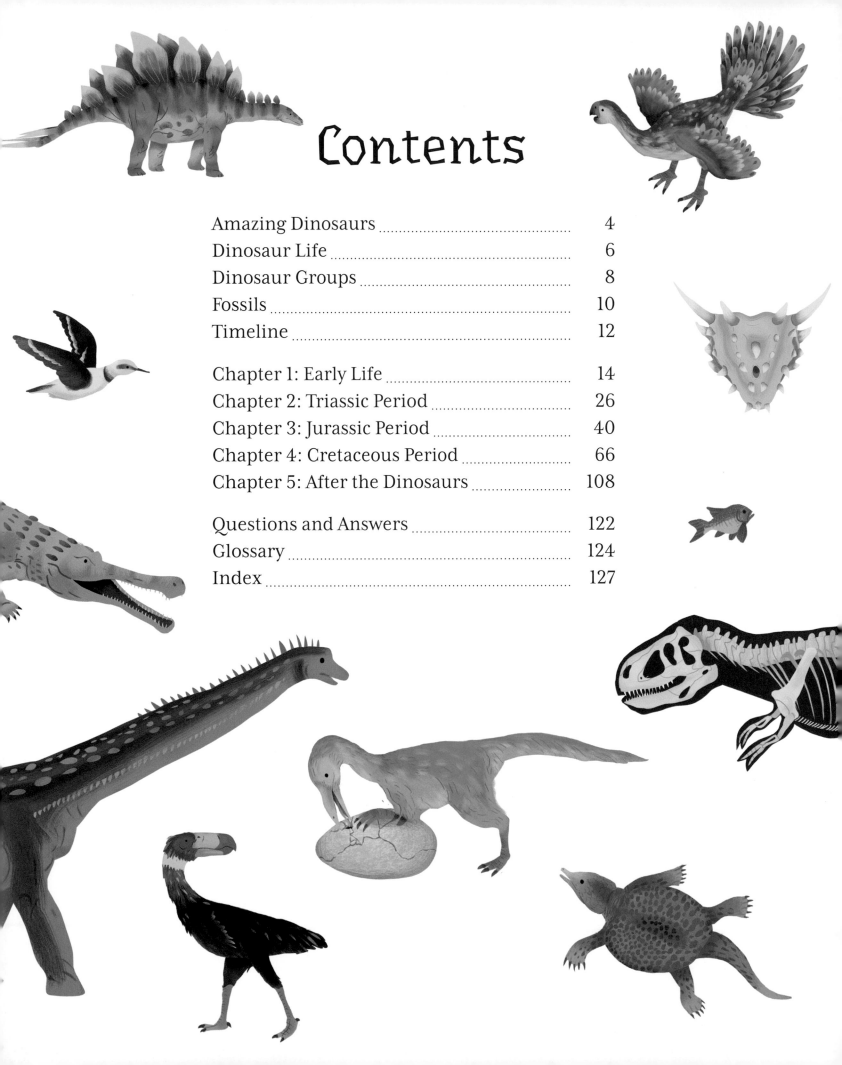

Amazing Dinosaurs 4

Dinosaur Life 6

Dinosaur Groups 8

Fossils 10

Timeline 12

Chapter 1: Early Life 14

Chapter 2: Triassic Period 26

Chapter 3: Jurassic Period 40

Chapter 4: Cretaceous Period 66

Chapter 5: After the Dinosaurs 108

Questions and Answers 122

Glossary 124

Index 127

Amazing Dinosaurs

Dinosaurs were an amazing group of reptiles, both fierce and peaceful, huge and tiny, speedy and lumbering. They walked the Earth from around 233 million years ago until 66 million years ago. Today's reptiles include crocodiles, lizards, and snakes. Most modern reptiles have skin covered by scales, breathe air using their lungs, and lay tough-shelled eggs on land. Dinosaurs shared these characteristics, although a few of them had feathers as well as scales. The very first reptiles lived around 312 million years ago. Over millions of years, reptiles slowly changed—or evolved—into many different groups, including flying reptiles known as pterosaurs; swimming reptiles such as mosasaurs; and the dinosaurs, which usually lived on land.

Over the 167 million years that dinosaurs hatched, ate, drank, slept, and fought, more than 1,000 dinosaur species evolved. A species is a group of animals that look similar and can make babies together. Evolution takes place because parents pass on their characteristics—such as a long neck—to their babies. A useful characteristic such as a longer neck, which allows a plant-eating dinosaur to reach higher branches than its rivals, gives that dinosaur a better chance of surviving until it is mature enough to have its own, longer-necked babies. These babies pass on their longer necks to their babies … and over time, the useful characteristic becomes more and more common. When a species has changed so much that it looks distinctly different, scientists call it a new species. In this way, a new species of extremely long-necked dinosaurs evolves.

As new species of dinosaurs evolved, others became extinct. Some species became extinct because larger, sharper-toothed dinosaurs evolved to kill them. Others became extinct because faster or taller dinosaurs evolved to steal their prey or eat their conifer trees. In the end, all the dinosaurs became extinct when a space rock, known as an asteroid, hit Earth. Yet we could say that some dinosaurs are alive and well today! Before the asteroid struck, some dinosaurs had evolved beaks, feathers, and wings—and flown into the sky as birds.

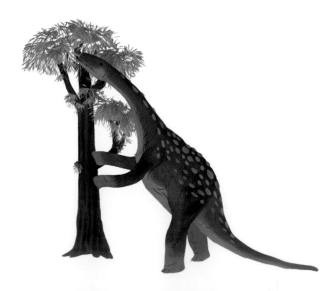

Opisthocoelicaudia was a plant-eating dinosaur that lived around 70 million years ago. In addition to its usefully long neck, it had a long, flexible tail that helped it balance as it fed on high branches.

Around 130 million years ago, two dinosaurs splash through a wetland in what is today central Spain. Hump-backed *Concavenator* tries to seize a frightened *Pelecanimimus* in its sharp-toothed jaws.

Dinosaur Life

Paleontologists are scientists who study the fossils of dinosaurs and other extinct living things. They have pieced together a picture of how dinosaurs looked and how they may have behaved. There are still many mysteries that may never be solved, including what kinds of noises dinosaurs made to show friendliness or fear.

DIFFERENT FROM THE REST

Dinosaurs had an advantage over other reptiles. Other reptiles have legs that sprawl to the sides, so they must wriggle their body from side to side when they run, making them both breathless and slower. Dinosaurs walked with their back legs directly beneath their body, so the legs could take longer strides and carry more weight. This allowed dinosaurs to be faster and grow bigger.

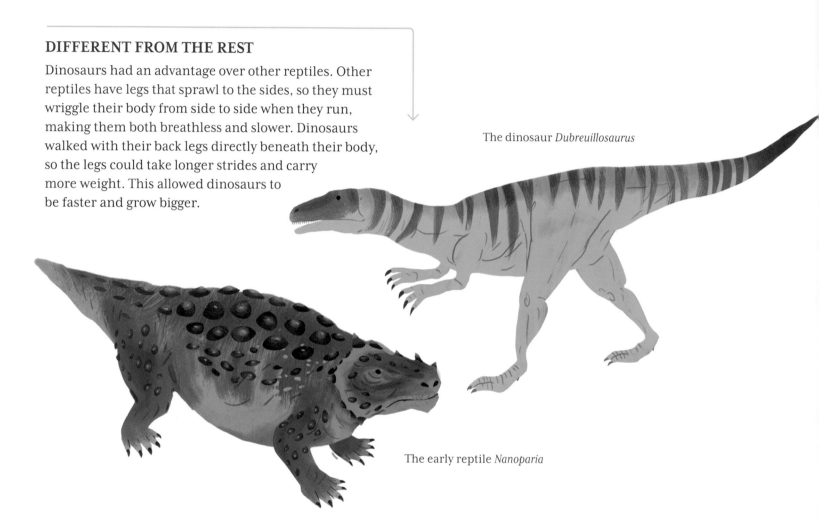

The dinosaur *Dubreuillosaurus*

The early reptile *Nanoparia*

Lucianovenator

MEAT AND PLANTS

The earliest dinosaurs were meat-eaters, also known as carnivores. Meat-eating dinosaurs preyed on many different animals, including insects, fish, amphibians, mammals, and reptiles, including dinosaurs. Over time, around two-thirds of dinosaurs evolved to be plant-eaters, also known as herbivores. They ate plant parts such as leaves, fruit, twigs, and bark.

LAYING EGGS

Like most reptiles and all birds, dinosaurs laid eggs. Female dinosaurs laid up to 30 eggs in a nest, which they scraped in the ground or built from piled-up mud and leaves. Some dinosaurs sat gently on their eggs to keep them warm, then watched over their young dinosaurs after they hatched. Yet some meat-eating dinosaurs buried their eggs safely, then walked away, leaving their sharp-clawed babies to care for themselves after hatching.

Oviraptor

Omeisaurus herd

LIVING TOGETHER

Although large meat-eaters probably hunted alone, many plant-eaters moved in a herd. Living in a group was safer, since all the dinosaurs could bite, claw, and kick a predator—or all run in different directions, leaving the predator unsure which to chase. Dinosaurs probably made calls to communicate with their herd. Some paleontologists think these calls included rumbles and booms.

SCALES AND FEATHERS

Most dinosaurs had skin covered by scales, which are small plates made of keratin. This tough material is also found in hair, horns, and hooves. Scales protected dinosaur skin from being damaged. A few dinosaurs had bigger, bonier plates known as scutes, which offered even better protection. Some meat-eating dinosaurs had feathers, which are also made of keratin. While early feathered dinosaurs had short, soft feathers for warmth, some later dinosaurs grew longer, stiffer feathers—and evolved into birds.

Oksoko

Panoplosaurus

Dinosaur Groups

Dinosaurs can be divided into groups based on their similarities. Dinosaurs that looked very similar are placed in the same species. Similar species are placed in larger groups such as families, which are placed in even larger groups, such as suborders. Many paleontologists group dinosaurs into four suborders: theropods, sauropodomorphs, cerapods, and thyreophorans.

Megalosaurus

THEROPODS

Most theropods were meat-eaters—and nearly all meat-eating dinosaurs were theropods. These dinosaurs usually walked on their back legs, freeing their shorter front limbs for grasping prey. Theropods had hollow bones, making them more lightweight. They usually had three main toes and three main fingers. Most feathered dinosaurs were in the theropod suborder, but some groups of theropods had scales. Theropods ranged from around 34 cm (13 in) to 14.3 m (47 ft) long.

SAUROPODOMORPHS

These dinosaurs were plant-eaters. They had long necks for reaching high or distant food, and long tails to balance the weight of their necks. Early sauropodomorphs walked on their back legs, but later sauropodomorphs were so big and heavy that they walked on all fours. The largest sauropodomorphs were the largest dinosaurs of all, reaching 35 m (114.8 ft) long.

Diplodocus

Triceratops

CERAPODS

The cerapods were plant-eaters, with hard, keratin-covered beaks for cutting twigs and stems. Their teeth had sharp ridges, which helped to mush plants. Some cerapods walked on two legs, and others walked on four. Cerapods included ceratopsians, which often had horns and neck frills; and pachycephalosaurs, which had domed skulls.

THYREOPHORANS

These plant-eaters had thick bony plates known as scutes, which protected them from attack. Due to the weight of their scutes, most thyreophorans walked on four, sturdy legs, with their front legs usually shorter than their back legs. Thyreophorans included stegosaurs, which had rows of tall scutes down their back; and ankylosaurs, which sometimes had a bony tail club.

Stegosaurus

Ankylosaurus

Pterodactylus

Gryposuchus

DINOSAUR RELATIVES

The dinosaurs were in the archosaur superorder of reptiles. These reptiles had the advantages of teeth set deep into sockets, so they did not fall out easily; and extra openings in their skulls, making them more lightweight. Other archosaurs included pterosaurs, which were flying reptiles; and pseudosuchians, which were crocodile-like reptiles. Today, the only surviving archosaurs are birds and crocodiles and their relatives.

Fossils

Fossils have taught us everything we know about dinosaurs and other extinct living things. Fossils are the preserved remains of animals and plants. Some, known as body fossils, preserve an animal's body—or parts of it. Others, known as trace fossils, preserve traces of the animal, such as its footprints or poop.

BODY FOSSILS

Most body fossils form when a dead animal is quickly covered with mud or sand, which can happen in water or in deserts. Usually, the animal's soft body parts, such as skin, fat, and muscle, rot away. It is the hard body parts—such as bones, teeth, and horns—that have the best chance of being preserved. More mud or sand pile on top of the body and, over thousands of years, harden into rocks such as mudstone and sandstone. Water seeps into the bones and teeth, turning them to rock as it deposits tough materials known as minerals.

Sometimes, an animal's body is preserved by a different method. Animals that lived in an icy climate, such as woolly mammoths, can be frozen. Many insects were fossilized by being covered in sticky tree resin that hardened into amber. Some animals were preserved by falling into tar (see page 116).

TRACE FOSSILS

Fossils of footprints, burrows, and nests can form when they are baked by the sun, then covered by sand or mud. Footprints are particularly useful trace fossils because they tell us how an animal walked or ran.

Paleontologists make guesses about which dinosaur made which footprints by comparing the number and sizes of toes with the fossils of feet found nearby. To make estimates of walking or running speed, paleontologists measure the distance between footprints as well as their depth. When several tracks are found together, paleontologists can figure out if the dinosaurs lived in a herd.

Fossilized poops, known as coprolites, preserve the remains of bones, shells, or leaves, telling paleontologists about an animal's diet and chewing habits. Paleontologists cannot always know which dinosaur made which coprolite, but there are clues in a coprolite's size, shape, and location.

A dinosaur dies on the seashore, sinks to the water bottom, then is quickly buried by sand and mud.

Beneath layers of rock, the dinosaur's bones and teeth are replaced by minerals.

The fossil is lifted by movements of the great plates of rock that form Earth's surface. The surrounding rock is worn away, revealing the fossil.

Paleontologists uncover fossils very carefully, documenting each bone and its position. By examining the shapes of a dinosaur's bones and teeth, paleontologists find out how the animal looked and how it might have behaved. They also examine the layers of rock around a fossil to discover its age.

Timeline

The first tiny, very simple living things appeared in the oceans around 3.5 billion years ago. Over millions and billions of years, these living things changed and developed—evolving into all the animals, plants, and other living things that we know today.

TIME PERIODS

Scientists divide Earth's history into periods of time. The beginnings and endings of these periods are marked by great events, such as widespread extinctions or big steps in animal development. The dinosaurs evolved in the Triassic Period (252–201 million years ago), dominated Earth in the Jurassic Period (201–145 million years ago), and were wiped out at the end of the Cretaceous Period (145–66 million years ago).

Ammonoids were shelled sea creatures that evolved around 409 million years ago. Ammonoids are used as "dating fossils," since the presence of a particular ammonoid species in a layer of rock helps paleontologists identify the time period.

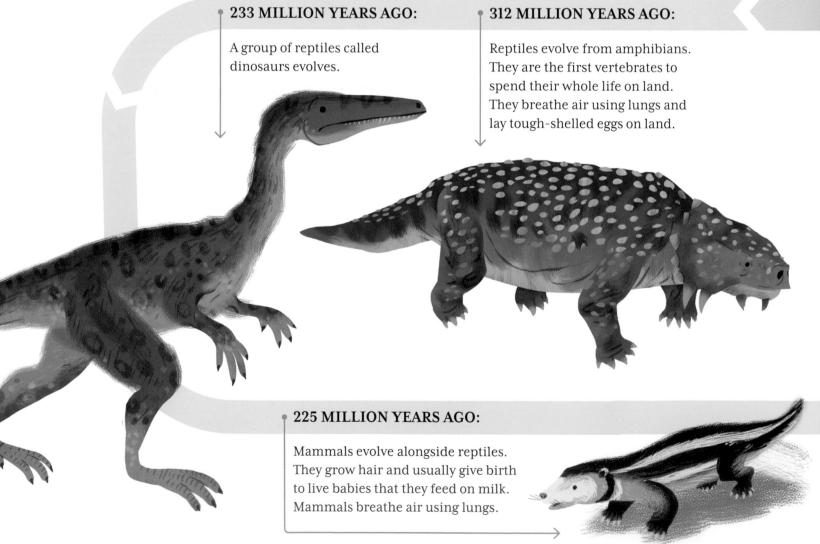

233 MILLION YEARS AGO:

A group of reptiles called dinosaurs evolves.

312 MILLION YEARS AGO:

Reptiles evolve from amphibians. They are the first vertebrates to spend their whole life on land. They breathe air using lungs and lay tough-shelled eggs on land.

225 MILLION YEARS AGO:

Mammals evolve alongside reptiles. They grow hair and usually give birth to live babies that they feed on milk. Mammals breathe air using lungs.

4.5 BILLION YEARS AGO:

Earth forms in the cloud of dust spinning around the young Sun.

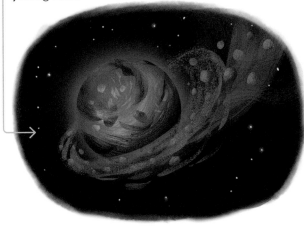

600 MILLION YEARS AGO:

Animals evolve in the oceans. The earliest animals are invertebrates, which means that they do not have a backbone. The majority of today's animals, from insects to jellyfish, are still invertebrates.

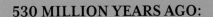

350 MILLION YEARS AGO:

Amphibians evolve from fish. They are among the earliest four-legged animals, called tetrapods. Most amphibians spend their early lives in water and breathe using gills, but they develop lungs and move onto land as adults.

530 MILLION YEARS AGO:

Fish evolve from invertebrates. They are the earliest animals with backbones, known as vertebrates. Fish breathe by taking oxygen from water using gills. They have fins and scale-covered skin.

72 MILLION YEARS AGO:

Birds evolve from theropod dinosaurs. They have feathers, wings, and beaks. Birds lay hard-shelled eggs on land and breathe air using lungs.

66 MILLION YEARS AGO:

Dinosaurs and most large animals become extinct after a space rock, known as an asteroid, hits Earth. Around 20 percent of animals survive, including small invertebrates, fish, amphibians, reptiles, mammals, and birds.

Early Life

Around 4.5 billion years ago, Earth formed from the dust swirling around the newborn Sun. The young Earth was sizzling hot. For around the first billion years, there was no life on Earth. Yet after Earth cooled enough for rain to fall and seas to flow, something extraordinary happened: The first life forms appeared in the oceans. These first living things were very tiny and simple, but over time they would evolve into all the living things on our planet, from plants and fungi to animals. Today, there are six groups of animals: invertebrates, fish, amphibians, reptiles, mammals, and birds. By the start of the Triassic Period (see page 26), the first four of these animal groups had evolved.

The first, simple animals evolved in the oceans around 600 million years ago. They were invertebrates, with no backbone or other internal skeleton. Invertebrates were the first animals to crawl out of the oceans onto land, around 420 million years ago. The first animals with backbones, known as vertebrates, were fish. They evolved from swimming invertebrates around 530 million years ago. Then, around 350 million years ago, amphibians evolved from fish. Amphibians were the first animals with four legs, known as tetrapods. All of today's tetrapods—amphibians, reptiles, mammals, and birds—are descended from those early tetrapods. This includes tetrapods that have lost their legs, such as snakes; evolved wings or flippers rather than legs; or learned to walk on two legs, such as humans. Like fish, amphibians laid jelly-like eggs in water and spent their early days in water, but as adults they developed lungs for breathing air and could survive on land, as long as they stayed damp. Amphibians were the first vertebrates to spend time on land.

Reptiles evolved from amphibians around 312 million years ago. Reptiles were the first vertebrates to spend all their time on land. They were born with lungs for breathing air, their scale-covered skin did not need to stay damp, and their tough-shelled eggs did not dry out on land. These characteristics helped reptiles begin to dominate the land.

The reptile *Bunostegos* lived in Africa around 252 million years ago. Its skin was protected by scales and bony plates. It died out in the wave of extinctions that marked the start of the Triassic Period.

Around 280 million years ago, the fish-eating amphibian *Eryops* is one of the largest predators in North America, growing up to 2 m (6.6 ft) long. Distracted by gripping its wriggling prey, *Eryops* fails to notice the approach of a rival predator, *Dimetrodon*, a reptile-like relative of mammals. The sight of *Dimetrodon*'s tall back sail may startle *Eryops* into dropping its prize.

Ediacaran Seafloor

Around 555 million years ago, South Australia was covered by ocean. Fossils of some of the earliest animals have been found in the region's Ediacaran Hills. These fossils are so important that the hills gave their name to a period of time, the Ediacaran, which lasted from 635 to 538 million years ago.

The Ediacaran Period saw the appearance of the first simple animals, which evolved from yet simpler ocean-dwelling life forms. All these early, strange-looking animals became extinct millions of years ago, but some of their descendants evolved into the animals we know today.

Ediacaran animals usually had a symmetrical, soft body without a shell or bones. Some were sessile, staying in one spot like modern animals such as corals, but others wriggled across the seafloor. With no mouth, Ediacaran animals did not prey on each other, instead absorbing tiny life forms or nutrients from the water or seafloor.

DICKINSONIA

Up to 1.4 m (4.6 ft) long, *Dickinsonia's* body was divided into segments, each filled with liquid that may have transported food through the animal. *Dickinsonia* probably soaked up tiny living things through its underside, as it moved slowly across the seafloor.

SPRIGGINA

Spriggina had a harder body than most Ediacarans, its many segments covered by tough plates. Its front segments were fused into a head, which may have contained a basic brain—possibly making *Spriggina* the first "intelligent" animal.

CHARNIA

Although it looked like a plant, *Charnia* was probably an animal that attached itself to the seafloor. Unlike plants, which make their own food from sunlight, it most likely fed by soaking up nutrients in the water.

CYCLOMEDUSA

Cyclomedusa may have been a single sessile animal or a colony of bacteria that lived together, forming a mat. Specimens range in size from 5 cm (2 in) to around 1 m (3.3 ft) across.

TRIBRACHIDIUM

Tribrachidium (meaning "three-armed" in Latin) had three arms, or lobes, twisted into a loose spiral. Although the arms did not move, as water flowed over them it was carried into three pits, where food particles collected.

PARVANCORINA

Only around 1 cm (2.5 in) long, *Parvancorina* (meaning "small anchor" in Latin) had a ridge down the middle of its body, with another, curving ridge at its head. It probably rested with its head facing into the current, which carried food particles to small openings.

Arthropleura

Up to 2.5 m (8.2 ft) long, *Arthropleura* was the largest land-dwelling invertebrate that ever lived. It was a millipede, a type of invertebrate with many jointed legs. Like today's invertebrates, including millipedes, insects, and jellyfish, it did not have a backbone or any other internal skeleton.

MOVING ONTO LAND

Until around 518 million years ago, all animals were invertebrates. Millipedes evolved around 420 million years ago from sea-dwelling invertebrates. To live on land, millipedes developed spiracles, which are holes that soak up oxygen from the air. Millipedes were among the first known animals to live on land, many millions of years before the first backboned animals crawled ashore.

Like insects, crabs, and spiders, millipedes are arthropods, which have a hard outer covering, known as an exoskeleton; a segmented body; and pairs of jointed legs. Millipedes are often called "living fossils" because they have changed little over millions of years. Today, there are more than 12,000 species of millipedes. Although millipede means "thousand legs" in Latin, most species have between 40 and 400 legs. *Arthropleura* had 28 to 32 body segments, with around 8 pairs of legs for every 6 segments.

GROWING GIANT

A fossilized track left by the millipede is 50 cm (20 in) wide. One fossilized exoskeleton—shed by the millipede as it grew—is estimated to have belonged to an *Arthropleura* that weighed 50 kg (110 lb). *Arthropleura* could evolve to be so large because it had few—if any— predators. In addition, when *Arthropleura* was alive, Earth's atmosphere contained much more oxygen— which animals' cells use to make energy—than it does today. This gave animals more fuel, resulting in many invertebrates growing much larger.

No one knows for sure what *Arthropleura* ate because fossilized mouthparts have never been found. Yet, if it had strong jaws for biting prey, they probably would have survived. This leads paleontologists to believe that—like most modern millipedes—*Arthropleura* ate plants and rotting material. *Arthropleura* became extinct around 290 million years ago, possibly due to climate change, as well as increasing competition from land-living vertebrates including amphibians and reptiles.

Arthropleura Facts

PHYLUM	Arthropods
CLASS	Diplopods
ORDER	Arthropleurids
SPECIES	*Arthropleura armata*
RANGE	North America and Europe
TIME PERIOD	345–290 million years ago
SIZE	1.9–2.5 m (6.2–8.2 ft) long

An *Arthropleura* hunts for rotting plants, while above its head darts a *Meganeura*. Related to modern dragonflies, *Meganeura* was one of the largest known flying insects, with a wingspan of up to 70 cm (28 in).

East Kirkton

Some of the earliest fossils of land-living tetrapods have been found in the rocks of Scotland's East Kirkton. The fossils are around 335 million years old. Tetrapods are four-limbed animals with backbones. Today's amphibians, reptiles, birds, and mammals evolved from early tetrapods.

The East Kirkton fossils show us how tetrapods adapted to life on land. Some of the tetrapods are amphibians, like modern frogs. Amphibians, which evolved from fish, were among the earliest tetrapods and the first to spend time on land. Most amphibians spend their early life in water, but then develop lungs and can live on land as adults.

Other East Kirkton fossils are of tetrapods that have features of both amphibians and reptiles. These fossils give glimpses of how reptiles evolved from amphibians, developing features such as scaly skin as they moved away from water and became the first fully land-living tetrapods.

BALANERPETON

Up to 50 cm (20 in) long, *Balanerpeton* was an amphibian. It laid eggs in water that hatched into water-dwelling larvae that took oxygen from water using gills. As an adult, *Balanerpeton* spent time on land, where it breathed by gulping air into its lungs.

KIRKTONECTA

Kirktonecta belonged to the microsaur group of small, sharp-toothed amphibians. It probably fed on insects and larvae caught in and around fresh water.

WESTLOTHIANA

Westlothiana was a reptile-like amphibian or possibly one of the very earliest reptiles. It had scaly skin and a lizard-like body. Since no eggs have been found, we cannot know if *Westlothiana* laid jelly-like eggs in water, like an amphibian, or tough-shelled eggs on land, like a reptile.

SILVANERPETON

Like *Westlothiana* and *Eldeceeon*, *Silvanerpeton* was a reptiliomorph, a tetrapod with reptile-like features. Yet its long, smooth-shaped body and short legs suggest it spent much of its time in water, where it snapped up invertebrates with its strong jaws.

BRIGANTIBUNUM

Brigantibunum was a type of spider often called a "daddy longlegs." These spiders have changed little since they evolved around 410 million years ago. Spiders are invertebrates, which were the first animals to live on land, around 425 million years ago.

ELDECEEON

Eldeceeon's long, strong legs suggest it lived entirely on land. Around 35 cm (14 in) long, *Eldeceeon* probably walked far and wide in search of insects, spiders, and possibly also plants to eat.

Hylonomus

Hylonomus was one of the very earliest reptiles. It lived in Canada around 312 million years ago. No more than 25 cm (10 in) long, _Hylonomus_ looked like a modern lizard. However, it was not closely related to lizards, which did not evolve until around 200 million years ago.

FOREST DWELLER

Hylonomus means "forest dweller" in ancient Greek. Its fossils have been found in a region that was covered by rain forest when _Hylonomus_ was alive. Gymnosperm trees and tall club mosses grew beside winding rivers, while ferns cloaked the ground.

During storms, the club mosses were often blown over, leaving their stumps to rot and hollow out. _Hylonomus_ crawled into these warm hollows for shelter. Several _Hylonomus_ fossils have been found inside the preserved stumps.

EARLY REPTILE

Hylonomus is currently the earliest reptile that paleontologists all agree is indeed a reptile. Earlier very reptile-like animals, such as _Westlothiana_ (see page 21), probably represent stages in the slow evolution between amphibians and reptiles.

Like most reptiles other than dinosaurs, _Hylonomus_ had legs that sprawled to the sides, so its body was held close to the ground and had to wriggle from side to side while running. This meant that, although _Hylonomus_ could scuttle quite fast, it had to stop to catch its breath frequently. It was probably safest for _Hylonomus_ not to stray far from the safety of the club moss stump it called home.

Like other very early reptiles, _Hylonomus_ was a meat-eater. It had slender jaws and small, sharp teeth that were suited to snapping up little invertebrates such as millipedes, spiders, and insects. When _Hylonomus_ was alive, insects included the ancestors of today's cockroaches, mayflies, and dragonflies, but there were not yet any beetles or bees.

Hylonomus itself was preyed on by large amphibians, such as _Baphetes_, which had needle-like teeth in its 30-cm- (12-in-) long skull.

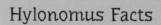

Hylonomus Facts	
CLASS	Reptiles
CLADE	Eureptiles
SPECIES	_Hylonomus lyelli_
RANGE	Canada in North America
TIME PERIOD	312 million years ago
SIZE	20–25 cm (8–10 in) long

Like other early reptiles, _Hylonomus_ had no openings in its skull bones apart from its eyes and nostrils. In contrast, dinosaurs had several openings in their skull (see page 36) that made them more lightweight.

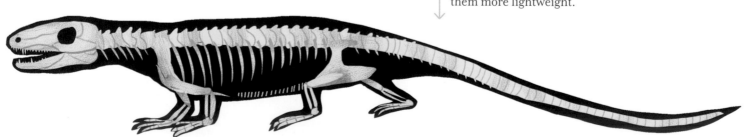

Hylonomus tries to snap up a *Palaeodictyoptera*, often known as a "six-winged insect." Unlike most modern insects, which have two pairs of wings, *Palaeodictyoptera* had a pair of wings on each of the three segments of their thorax (the area between the abdomen and head). The front pair (here shown in yellow) was much smaller than the two back pairs.

Pareiasaurs

These plant-eaters were the largest reptiles of the Permian Period. They were named pareiasaurs (meaning "cheek lizards" in ancient Greek) due to their broad cheek bones. They had short, thick legs; a small head; and a stocky body protected by bony plates, overlaid with horn, called scutes.

SCUTOSAURUS

This reptile was named "shield lizard" for its covering of shield-like, bumpy scutes. Its broad cheek bones ended in spikes. Short-legged and heavy-bodied, *Scutosaurus* relied on its scutes for protection from sharp-toothed mammal ancestors such as *Inostrancevia*.

BUNOSTEGOS

Bunostegos (meaning "knobbly cover" in ancient Greek) had large, bony, skin-covered knobs on its head. Knobblier individuals might have had more success at mating time. *Bunostegos* had a more upright stance than other reptiles of its time, with its legs held beneath its body rather than splayed to the sides, allowing it to run more easily.

NANOPARIA

One of the smallest pareiasaurs, *Nanoparia* was only around 60 cm (24 in) long and weighed 8 to 10 kg (18 to 22 lb). Its broad body, protected by a shell-like covering of scutes, has led some paleontologists to believe that *Nanoparia* was closely related to turtles, which evolved in the Late Jurassic Period.

ARGANACERAS

Arganaceras's broad snout was decorated by a small horn made from bone. This was not large enough for defending the reptile against attackers, so it may have been a feature that helped *Arganaceras* recognize other members of its species among the herds of plant-eaters.

PAREIASAURUS

Like other pareiasaurs, this reptile had leaf-shaped teeth, which are an ideal shape for biting through tough plant material such as stems, twigs, and leaves. The bony roof of its mouth also bore teeth to grind down food. *Pareiasaurus's* legs were thick and heavily muscled to carry its weight of up to 600 kg (1,300 lb).

Pareiasaur Facts

CLASS	Reptiles
SUBCLASS	Parareptiles
ORDER	Procolophonomorphs
RANGE	Worldwide
TIME PERIOD	265–252 million years ago
SIZE	0.6–3 m (2–9.8 ft) long

ELGINIA

This pareiasaur was named after Elgin in Scotland, where its fossils have been found. During the Permian Period, this region was dry and sandy. *Elginia's* skull was adorned with 40 horns or blunter knobs. Like a male deer today, a male *Elginia* probably showed off its horns to attract females and intimidate smaller-horned males.

Triassic Period

The beginning and end of the Triassic Period (252–201 million years ago) were marked by disaster. At the beginning of the period, huge volcanic eruptions raised Earth's temperature, leading to the extinction of up to 90 percent of all animal species. At the end of the Triassic Period, changes in climate again led to the extinction of an uncountable number of water- and land-living species. Yet these extinctions allowed the surviving animals to flourish. The survivors could take advantage of unused resources and move into new habitats. These opportunities allowed them to adapt, to change—and to evolve.

Some reptiles survived the extinctions that began the Triassic Period. Reptiles went on to become the most common land animals, with several amazing new groups evolving. One new group of reptiles was the strong-toothed archosaurs. Some archosaurs, known as pterosaurs, evolved wings and became the first backboned animals to fly. At around the same time, another group of archosaurs evolved: dinosaurs. These archosaurs had an upright stance that let them run fast. This advantage would help them become Earth's dominant land animals— but not until the following Jurassic Period.

During the Triassic Period, Earth did not look as it does today. Earth's surface is formed by giant plates of rock, known as tectonic plates. These plates move very slowly, pressing together, pulling apart, or moving past each other. Over millions of years, this has changed the shapes of the continents, pushed up mountains, and caused earthquakes and volcanoes. During the Triassic Period, all the continents were joined in one supercontinent, known as Pangea. The interior of Pangea was a hot, dry desert, but the coasts and polar areas were milder and wetter. Here there were forests of conifer, cycad, and ginkgo trees, as well as thickly growing ferns and horsetails. Grasses and other flowering plants were yet to evolve.

Living 216–201 million years ago, *Coelophysis* was one of the earliest known dinosaurs. Like most very early dinosaurs, it was a small, slim hunter that walked on its back legs.

In Late Triassic Germany, the dinosaur *Liliensternus* attacks the gentle plant-eater *Plateosaurus*. Around 5 m (16.4 ft) long, *Liliensternus* was a relative of later fierce dinosaurs such as *Tyrannosaurus*. *Plateosaurus* was an early sauropodomorph, a group of long-necked dinosaurs that included giants such as *Diplodocus*.

Tethys Ocean

During the Triassic Period, the vast Tethys Ocean covered parts of southern China, where it left behind countless fossils. By 235 million years ago, although dinosaurs had not begun to stalk the land, marine reptiles ruled this ancient ocean.

Reptiles evolved on land, but about 300 million years ago, some adapted to life in the ocean. A few groups, such as ichthyosaurs, became so suited to the ocean—with a streamlined body and flipper-like limbs—that they never returned to land, giving birth to live young in the water. Others probably went ashore to lay eggs.

During the Triassic Period, there were several hundred species of marine reptiles. Most became extinct, along with the dinosaurs, at the end of the Cretaceous Period. Today, out of around 12,000 species of reptiles, only about 100 live in the ocean, including sea turtles, saltwater crocodiles, sea snakes, and the marine iguana.

ANSHUNSAURUS

Up to 3.5 m (11.5 ft) long, this thalattosaur (meaning "sea lizard" in ancient Greek) swam with flicks of its long, flattened tail. Its broad teeth were suited to crushing the shells of animals such as ammonites.

GUIZHOUICHTHYOSAURUS

Named for the Chinese province of Guizhou, this ichthyosaur (meaning "fish lizard") swam with a wriggling motion. Over 6 m (20 ft) long, it had powerful jaws suited to grasping other large reptiles.

PSEPHOCHELYS

A little like a modern turtle, this reptile had a wide shell, made from fused bony plates, covering its back. Between dives to find shellfish, it breathed air into its lungs at the water surface.

LARIOSAURUS

Lariosaurus had front limbs that were adapted into paddles, but its back limbs retained toes. Its long, thin teeth formed a "trap" to catch fish.

KEICHOUSAURUS

Like other pachypleurosaurs, *Keichousaurus* had webbed feet and a long, slim body and neck, which were unsuited to crawling ashore to lay eggs. Its pointed snout and small, sharp teeth suggest it was a fish-eater.

PLACODUS

Since it had legs rather than flippers, *Placodus* probably spent time on the shore, where it may have laid eggs. Stocky and heavy boned, it dived easily to the seafloor, where it plucked hard-shelled prey with its protruding, chisel-like front teeth.

29

Eudimorphodon

Eudimorphodon was one of the earliest known pterosaurs. Close relatives of dinosaurs, pterosaurs (meaning "wing lizards" in ancient Greek) were flying reptiles that evolved around 228 million years ago—and died out along with the dinosaurs, around 66 million years ago.

WING LIZARD

Like all pterosaurs, *Eudimorphodon* had an extremely long fourth finger on each hand. Its wings were flaps of skin that stretched from this finger to its back legs. The wings were strengthened by muscles and tough, cordlike tissues, which helped *Eudimorphodon* to flap powerfully. The other three, clawed fingers of each hand stuck out at the front of the wing. In addition, an extra wrist bone, called the pteroid, helped to support the front edge of the wing.

A pterosaur's body and head were kept warm by a covering of fluffy, hairlike pycnofibers. Like feathers and hair, these contained keratin. Pycnofibers were similar to the soft feathers found on early dinosaurs and to the short feathers that modern birds have next to their skin.

When on land, *Eudimorphodon* walked on all fours, balancing on its back feet and the three short fingers of its hands. However, *Eudimorphodon*'s legs were not long enough for it to walk far. To take off, the pterosaur probably used all four limbs to make a standing jump into the air.

Eudimorphodon Facts

CLASS	Reptiles
ORDER	Pterosaurs
FAMILY	Eudimorphodontidae
SPECIES	*Eudimorphodon ranzii*
RANGE	Italy in Europe
DIET	210–203 million years ago
SIZE	0.9–1.1 m (3–3.6 ft) long

DIVING FOR FISH

Eudimorphodon lived along sea coasts. It flew over the ocean as it watched the waves for fish and other small sea creatures—then dived to the water surface to seize prey with its beaklike jaws. *Eudimorphodon*'s name means "true two-shaped teeth" in ancient Greek. It had 110 teeth squeezed into its 6-cm- (2.4-in-) long jaws. At the front of the mouth were long, fanglike teeth suited to grasping slippery fish. At the back were smaller, flatter teeth with up to five bumps, known as cusps. These crushed the shells of sea creatures such as ammonites.

Eudimorphodon's skull had several openings, and the rest of its bones were slender and hollow, making its skeleton lightweight and suited to flight. Its long tail may have had a diamond-shaped flap of skin and tissue at its tip, which helped with steering.

During the Late Triassic Period, *Eudimorphodon* was one of the most common pterosaurs in the region that is today Italy.

Cynodonts

Around 260 million years ago, cynodonts evolved alongside reptiles. Like today's mammals, cynodonts (meaning "dog teeth") had strong jaws with sharp teeth for cutting and flat teeth for grinding. They probably also grew fur. All modern mammals, from kangaroos to humans, are descended from early cynodonts.

THRINAXODON

Like other cynodonts, *Thrinaxodon* had a skull with mammal-like features. It had wide cheek bones, giving room for stronger jaw muscles, a feature that lets mammals chew their food thoroughly—unlike reptiles. The braincase bulged at the back of *Thrinaxodon's* skull. Although cynodonts still had small, reptile-like brains, an enlarged braincase allowed mammals to develop large brains.

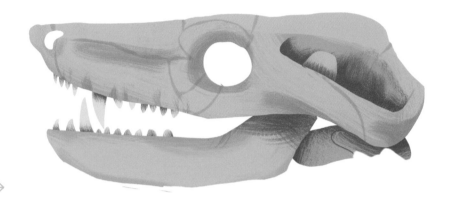

DIADEMODON

Around the size of a small cow, this cynodont had sharp, pointed side teeth (canines) and heavily ridged back teeth. This range of teeth suggests *Diademedon* was an omnivore, eating both small animals and plants, including possibly seaweeds it collected from shallow water.

MEGAZOSTRODON

Fossils of *Megazostrodon's* skull tell us that it had a larger brain than earlier cynodonts. The largest parts of its brain were those that process sounds and smells, suggesting that *Megazostrodon* was nocturnal. Only 10 cm (4 in) long, this cynodont probably hunted insects.

CYNOGNATHUS

Up to 1.2 m (3.9 ft) long, *Cynognathus* was a wide-jawed, strong-bodied predator. Its whiskers helped it sense air currents made by moving prey. *Cynognathus's* front legs sprawled to the sides like a reptile's, but its back legs were erect beneath its body, like a mammal's.

OLIGOKYPHUS

Little *Oligokyphus* fed on seeds and nuts, standing on its back legs to reach into shrubs and trees. Females probably laid eggs, like their reptile ancestors but unlike nearly all modern mammals. After hatching, babies sucked their mother's milk, as mammal babies do today.

MASSETOGNATHUS

Massetognathus was a plant-eater, using its chisel-like front teeth (incisors) for biting and its ridged back teeth (molars) for grinding roots and stems. Around the size of a fox, *Massetognathus* sheltered in a burrow, probably with its family.

Cynodont Facts

SUPERCLASS	Tetrapods
SUBCLASS	Synapsids
CLADE	Eutheridonts
RANGE	Worldwide
TIME PERIOD	260–120 million years ago
SIZE	0.1–2 m (0.3–6.6 ft) long

33

Ischigualasto

By 231 million years ago, some of the world's first dinosaurs were hunting across the plains of South America. Fossils of these early dinosaurs, along with other reptiles, have been discovered in Ischigualasto, in Argentina.

During the Triassic Period, the Ischigualasto area was a green plain where rivers wound their way to the ocean. Flowering plants did not yet exist, but plentiful rain watered tall coniferous trees, which reproduce by making seeds in cones; as well as ferns, which release tiny spores to make new plants.

Like other early dinosaurs, the Ischigualasto dinosaurs were smaller than some of their later relatives. They walked on their back legs. Most were meat-eaters, preying on smaller reptiles, amphibians, invertebrates, and fish.

EODROMAEUS

One of the earliest known dinosaurs, *Eodromaeus* was probably an ancestor of theropods such as *Tyrannosaurus*. Just 1.2 m (4 ft) long and lightly built, it could run fast in pursuit of insects and small reptiles.

PANPHAGIA

The first dinosaurs were meat-eaters, but the dinosaur *Panphagia* ate both animals and plants. Its front teeth were long for slicing flesh, while its shorter back teeth were ribbed for mashing plants. An ancestor of long-necked plant-eaters such as *Diplodocus*, *Panphagia* was probably one of the earliest dinosaurs to eat plants.

SILLOSUCHUS

Despite its dinosaur-like appearance, *Sillosuchus* was not a dinosaur but a pseudosuchian reptile, related to modern crocodiles. Up to 10 m (33 ft) long, it was far larger than any Triassic dinosaur. It cropped plants with its toothless beak.

HYPERODAPEDON

A rhyncosaur (meaning "beak lizard" in ancient Greek) rather than a dinosaur, *Hyperodapedon* used its beaklike jaws and huge front teeth for chopping ferns.It dug up roots with its strong back legs.

HERRERASAURUS

The largest dinosaur found at Ischigualasto, *Herrerasaurus* could grow to more than 5 m (16.4 ft) long. It preyed on smaller dinosaurs as well as rhyncosaurs and small pseudosuchians.

AETOSAUROIDES

Like *Sillosuchus*, plant-eating *Aetosauroides* was a pseudosuchian. Rows of bony scutes protected its body from the teeth and claws of large, fast-moving dinosaurs such as *Herrerasaurus*.

Eoraptor

**One of the very first dinosaurs, *Eoraptor* was named "dawn snatcher,"
which refers to its early evolution and its grasping hands. This dinosaur's fossils have
been found in Argentina's Ischigualasto, along with those of other early dinosaurs.**

UNDECIDED DINOSAUR

Paleontologists do not agree on whether *Eoraptor* was an
early theropod or an early sauropodomorph. Theropods
later evolved into a wide range of mostly meat-eating
dinosaurs that walked on their back legs. Yet early
theropods were much smaller than some of their later
relatives. Sauropodomorphs later evolved into huge, long-
necked, long-tailed plant-eaters that walked on all fours.
However, early sauropodomorphs were small, walked on
their back legs, and ate both meat and plants.

In fact, the earliest theropods and sauropodomorphs were
very closely related: They shared a common ancestor who
had lived not long before, so they were only just starting
to develop different characteristics. Both groups were
saurischian dinosaurs, which had hips in which two
downward-pointing bones—the pubis and ischium—jutted
in opposite directions, one forward and one back.

At just 1 m (3.3 ft) tall and weighing 10 kg (22 lb), *Eoraptor*
was small. It walked on its back legs. It probably had an
omnivorous ("all eating") diet of both small animals and
plants. The teeth in its upper jaw were sharp and jagged
edged for biting prey, like those of theropods. Yet the teeth
in its lower jaw were leaf-shaped for mashing plants, like
those of sauropodomorphs.

Eoraptor Facts

CLASS	Reptiles
SUPERORDER	Dinosaurs
ORDER	Saurischians
SPECIES	*Eoraptor lunensis*
RANGE	Argentina in South America
DIET	231–228 million years ago
SIZE	1–1.7 m (3.3–5.6 ft) long

GRASPING PREY

Eoraptor could run fast in pursuit of prey on its long back
legs, leaving its shorter front limbs free to grasp prey. It
had five fingers on each hand, but fingers four and five
were much shorter than the others and not useful for
gripping. While *Eoraptor*'s ancestors probably had five
useful fingers, its descendants may have lost fingers four
and five. *Eoraptor*'s three main fingers were strong and
had long claws for piercing and ripping small animals.

Dinosaurs (and their pterosaur and pseudosuchian
relatives) had more openings in their skulls than other
reptiles (see page 22), making them more lightweight.
These openings included the antorbital fenestra in
front of the eye, the lateral temporal fenestra behind
the eye, and the mandibular fenestra in the lower jaw.

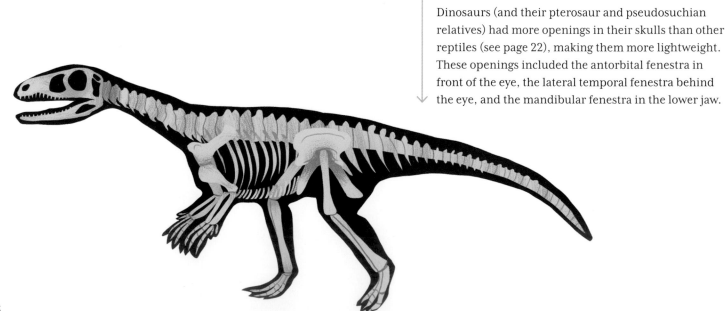

In Late Triassic Argentina, *Eoraptor* sprints after a scuttling *Probainognathus*. This small cynodont fed on invertebrates—and was no match for the speed and size of *Eoraptor*.

Coelophysids

These early dinosaurs were theropods, a group of dinosaurs with hollow bones and clawed fingers and toes. Later theropods include tyrannosaurs and birds. Coelophysids were meat-eaters with long snouts and slender, lightweight skeletons suited to running fast on their back legs. Like other early theropods, they may have had a fluffy covering for warmth.

CAMPOSAURUS

Like modern predators, *Camposaurus* had large, forward-facing eyes. This eye placement provides "binocular vision," when the two eyes work together so the predator's brain can judge the distance to fast-moving prey. *Camposaurus's* slender snout, with many small teeth, was suited to snapping small prey such as lizard-like reptiles.

COELOPHYSIS

Like its relatives, *Coelophysis* had very sharp, backward-curving teeth to trap wriggling lizard-like prey. *Coelophysis's* teeth also had horizontal ridges, which might have helped it grip slippery fish that it snatched from rivers and wetlands.

PROCOMPSOGNATHUS

Procompsognathus was around 1 m (3.3 ft) long but weighed only 1.3 kg (2.9 lb). It had long back legs and a stiff tail, which helped with balance when running. Its short arms and large, clawed hands were used for grasping prey. Its skull had several large openings, known as fenestrae, which made it lightweight.

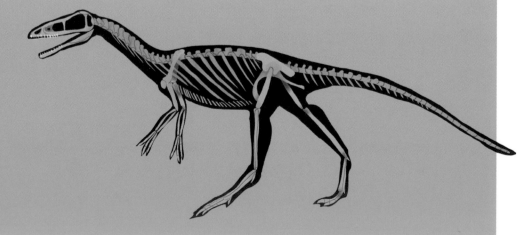

LUCIANOVENATOR

This dinosaur was named after Luciano Leyes, who first discovered its fossils in Argentina, in 2017. *Lucianovenator's* long, flexible neck helped with grabbing prey during a chase, as well as reaching among plants or rocks for hiding prey.

SEGISAURUS

Only one fossil of *Segisaurus* has ever been discovered, in Arizona, USA. When it died, the *Segisaurus* was crouching on the ground among sand dunes. Paleontologists think that it was sheltering from a sandstorm but was covered by sand.

MEGAPNOSAURUS

The fossils of more than 30 *Megapnosauruses* were found together, suggesting that this dinosaur hunted in packs to kill large animals such as plant-eating dinosaurs. Another possibility is that the *Megapnosauruses* were not a pack but happened to be drinking from the same water hole when they were killed by a flash flood.

Coelophysid Facts

CLASS	Reptiles
SUPERORDER	Dinosaurs
SUBORDER	Theropods
RANGE	North America, South America, Europe, Africa, and Asia
TIME PERIOD	228–183 million years ago
SIZE	1–3 m (3.3–9.8 ft) long

Jurassic Period

During the Jurassic Period (201–145 million years ago), dinosaurs were the dominant land animals: They were the most common animals in most land habitats, and large dinosaurs were the largest animals in any habitat. The dinosaurs' success was helped by the extinction of many other reptile groups at the end of the Triassic Period. The Jurassic Period saw the dinosaurs adapting to a range of habitats and lifestyles— and the evolution of hundreds of new species.

There were four main groups of dinosaurs: theropods, sauropodomorphs, cerapods, and thyreophorans (see pages 8–9). Primitive theropods and sauropodomorphs had evolved during the Triassic Period. During the Jurassic Period, the meat-eating theropods became the largest, fiercest, and fastest predators on land. Some groups of theropods began to evolve more birdlike characteristics. This was the start of the process that would result—during the following Cretaceous Period—in the first true birds. In the Jurassic Period, sauropodomorphs became the planet's most widespread plant-eaters, with many growing to immense sizes—and becoming the largest animals yet to have walked on land. The Jurassic Period also saw the evolution of the first cerapods and thyreophorans. These plant-eaters began to take on many different forms, from spiky stegosaurs to tanklike nodosaurs.

In the Jurassic Period, the continents began to drift apart, forming two main landmasses, known today as Laurasia (including North America, Europe, and most of Asia) and Gondwana (including South America, Africa, Antarctica, Australia, and parts of Asia). Animals that evolved on one of those landmasses were often able to spread across them. The climate was warmer and wetter than today. Even at the poles, it was so warm that forests of conifer trees could grow. Conifers, which make their seeds in woody cones, were the period's most widespread plants.

Hesperosaurus was a stegosaur, one of a group of thyreophorans that lived throughout Laurasia. Stegosaurs also crossed a bridge of land into North Africa.

During the Jurassic Period, Antarctica was closer to the equator and much warmer than today. Its forests were home to the crested theropod dinosaur *Cryolophosaurus*, as well as the plant-eating sauropodomorph *Glacialisaurus*, which grew to around 6 m (20 ft) long.

Shaximiao

In 1972, dinosaur bones were unearthed near Zigong in China. Since then, over 8,000 pieces of bone have been discovered at the site, which was named Shaximiao. These fossils let us build up a picture of life in the area 165 million years ago.

In the Jurassic Period, the Shaximiao area was forested. A large river swept dead dinosaurs toward a lake, where the bodies were swiftly buried in mud, then fossilized. Paleontologists think that this geography explains the high number of fossils found here.

The many trees provided food for herds of sauropodomorph dinosaurs: large plant-eaters with long necks and long tails. Despite their similar diets and body shapes, different species of sauropodomorphs probably did not compete with each other for food, since each had a different length of neck, allowing it to feed on leaves at a different height from its relatives.

OMEISAURUS

Named after Mount Omei, a sacred mountain close to where it was found, this dinosaur was a sauropodomorph. Up to 20 m (66 ft) long, it was protected from predators by its size and its habit of moving in a herd.

AGILISAURUS

This small cerapod dinosaur used its hard beak to crop low-growing plant material, which it mashed with its ridged teeth. When escaping from predators, it ran fast on its long back legs, but it may have walked on all fours when browsing for food.

DATOUSAURUS

Datousaurus was closely related to *Omeisaurus*. The two sauropodomorphs did not compete with each other for food because *Datousaurus* had a shorter neck and stronger, larger jaws, suggesting that it fed on tougher, lower plants.

XUANHANOSAURUS

A meat-eater in the theropod suborder, this dinosaur grew to 4.5 m (15 ft) long. For a theropod, *Xuanhanosaurus* had unusually long, strong arms, which it used for grasping and grappling with prey, such as small stegosaurs.

HUAYANGOSAURUS

Up to 4 m (13 ft) long, *Huayangosaurus* was a small, early stegosaur. Like its famous relative *Stegosaurus*, it had a double row of plates along its back and a spiked tail, which it flicked at the legs of attackers.

ANGUSTINARIPTERUS

Angustinaripterus was a pterosaur, one of a group of flying reptiles closely related to dinosaurs. It had crisscrossing, needle-like teeth for trapping small prey. Its wingspan was around 1.6 m (5.2 ft) across.

Scelidosaurus

This dinosaur was one of the first thyreophorans, which means "shield bearers" in ancient Greek. The body of a thyreophoran had many bony plates, known as scutes, which could protect it from attack. Later thyreophorans included stegosaurs and ankylosaurs. *Scelidosaurus* had much lighter, smaller plates than its descendants. It lived in the British Isles.

Scelidosaurus's largest, sharpest scutes were on its vulnerable neck, where a single deep bite from a predator would have been deadly. Although there were gaps between this dinosaur's scutes, so that they did not form a continuous shield, they made *Scelidosaurus* a prickly and difficult meal.

SHIELDING SCUTES

Like all dinosaurs, even those that also had feathers, *Scelidosaurus* had scales. These are small, hard plates that grow from the top layer of skin. They are made of keratin, also known as horn, a material also found in human nails and hair, cow horns and hooves, and bird feathers and beaks. In addition to its scales, *Scelidosaurus* had scutes. Unlike scales, scutes grow from deep in the skin. Made of bone, with a covering of keratin over the skin, they are larger and harder than scales. Today, scutes are found in reptiles such as crocodiles.

There were hundreds of scutes, of different sizes and shapes, over *Scelidosaurus*'s head, back, and tail. The scutes were in rows, with larger scutes shaped like horns or spikes, which would have made it extremely difficult for a predator—such as the local theropod *Megalosaurus*—to take a bite.

EATING LEAVES

Scelidosaurus fed on low-growing leaves of ferns and conifers, using its hard, keratin-covered beak to rip them from branches. This dinosaur walked on four legs, but may have reared up on it back legs to reach higher leaves. Before swallowing food, the dinosaur probably mashed it a little with the long, triangular teeth that lined the backs of its jaws. *Scelidosaurus*'s simple jaw joint meant that it was not capable of complex chewing, but could make little up-and-down movements of its teeth.

Some paleontologists think that, like modern cows, *Scelidosaurus* fermented the food in its stomach. This is when tough plant material is broken down by tiny living things known as bacteria that make their home in the stomach. The bacteria take what they need from the food, leaving the rest of the nutrients to be soaked up into the animal's blood.

Scelidosaurus Facts

CLASS	Reptiles
SUPERORDER	Dinosaurs
SUBORDER	Thyreophorans
SPECIES	*Scelidosaurus harrisonii*
RANGE	British Isles in Europe
TIME PERIOD	196–183 million years ago
SIZE	3.8–4 m (12.5–13 ft) long

Stegosaurs

These large, slow-moving plant-eaters had rows of tall, spiky scutes along their back. The scutes, which left most of the body unprotected, would have been almost useless in battle. Stegosaurs relied on their spiked tail—known as a thagomizer—to defend themselves.

STEGOSAURUS

Stegosaurus (meaning "roof lizard" in ancient Greek) had a small brain compared with its huge body, so it probably had a simple lifestyle, wandering from shrub to shrub to eat leaves. The rows of scutes along its back may have helped to attract a mate or—since they made the stegosaur seem taller—frightened away predators.

MIRAGAIA

Miragaia had two rows of paired upright plates and spikes along its neck, back, and tail. Like the scutes of other stegosaurs, these were not attached to the rest of the skeleton since they grew from the dinosaur's skin. *Miragaia* had the longest neck of any stegosaur, containing 17 bones, called vertebrae, which allowed it to reach higher branches.

LORICATOSAURUS

Loricatosaurus could swivel its body and flick its tail to strike an attacker—such as the huge *Megalosaurus*—with its sharp-spiked thagomizer. Many stegosaur fossils have injured tail spikes, suggesting that they gave blows powerful enough to shatter the legs of predators.

HESPEROSAURUS

Like other stegosaurs, *Hesperosaurus* had no front teeth, instead using a horn-covered, hard-edged beak for cropping low-growing plants. Up to 6.5 m (21.3 ft) long, this stegosaur weighed as much as 5 tonnes (5.5 US tons)—more than two family cars.

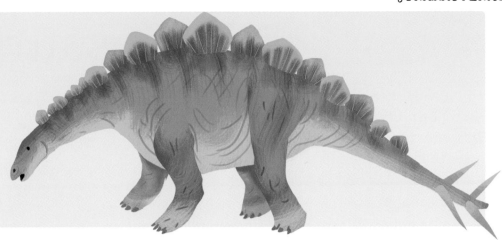

DACENTRURUS

Dacentrurus (meaning "very sharp tail") had a particularly effective thagomizer: Its spikes had sharp cutting edges at the front and back. The dinosaur's fossils were first found in 1874, when it was named *Omosaurus* (meaning "upper arm lizard") due to its long arm bones. It was renamed when it was realized that the first name was already taken by a crocodile-like reptile.

KENTROSAURUS

In addition to the plates and spikes along its back and tail, *Kentrosaurus* had a long spike on each shoulder. These could have protected *Kentrosaurus's* vital head and neck area, particularly if it crouched when attacked.

Stegosaur Facts

CLASS	Reptiles
SUPERORDER	Dinosaurs
SUBORDER	Thyreophorans
RANGE	North America, Europe, Africa, and Asia
TIME PERIOD	165–125 million years ago
SIZE	4–10 m (13–32.8 ft) long

Dilophosaurus

Dilophosaurus was one of the earliest large theropods. Like most later theropods, such as *Tyrannosaurus*, it was a sharp-toothed meat-eater that walked on its back legs. During the Early Jurassic Period, it was the largest known land animal in North America. With an adult weight of about 400 kg (88 lb), *Dilophosaurus* probably gained around 35 kg (77 lb)—the weight of a 10-year-old child—per year during its early life.

TWO-CRESTED LIZARD

The name *Dilophosaurus* comes from the ancient Greek words for "two-crested lizard." This dinosaur had two arched bone crests on its skull, which were probably made larger by keratin that has not survived in the fossils discovered so far. The crests were too thin and breakable to have any use in capturing prey or battling with rival *Dilophosauruses*. It is likely that the crests—which may have been brightly patterned—were shown off to attract a mate, just as some species of modern lizard display their bright crest or throat today.

JURASSIC KILLER

With its large skull, long front teeth, and strong neck, *Dilophosoaurus* was capable of killing any Jurassic plant-eating dinosaur it came across. Like today's big cats, it may have killed prey with one powerful bite to the neck or head. This dinosaur was also slender and agile enough to capture small prey, such as cynodonts.

Dilophosaurus's arms were longer and more powerful than those of some later theropods. It had four fingers on each hand, although the fourth was extremely small, clawless, and probably not movable. It may have been vestigial, which means it was a body structure that, as the animal evolved, began to have no use. The first three fingers on each hand had sharp, curved claws.

Like other theropods, *Dilophosaurus* had limited movement in its wrists, so it was unable to twist and turn its hands. Therefore, the palms of its hands faced toward each other. Yet this predator was able to use its hands to grasp prey and to pull small animals to its mouth.

Dilophosaurus Facts

CLASS	Reptiles
SUPERORDER	Dinosaurs
SUBORDER	Theropods
SPECIES	*Dilophosaurus wetherilli*
RANGE	North America
TIME PERIOD	193 million years ago
SIZE	6–7 m (19.7–23 ft) long

Dilophosaurus could probably run at up to 32 km/h (20 miles per hour) on its long, strong back legs. It was fast enough to catch local plant-eating dinosaurs, which included early thyreophorans and sauropodomorphs.

Morrison

Today, the quiet town of Morrison lies in the state of Colorado, USA. On this spot 150 million years ago, fierce theropod dinosaurs hunted. Slowly, sand and mud were deposited by rivers and streams. Sandstones and mudstones formed, creating the fossil-rich rocks of the Morrison Formation.

In the Jurassic Period, the Morrison region was warm and low-lying, a place of swamps and slow rivers. Plants such as ginkgos, cycads, and horsetail rushes grew by the water, providing food for plant-eaters from tall sauropodomorphs to shy mammals.

Some meat-eating dinosaurs found plentiful food—including fish, frogs, turtles, and bugs—in the shallow water or on muddy banks. Others fed on the insects, mammals, and smaller dinosaurs that scurried nearby.

CERATOSAURUS

Ceratosaurus (meaning "horn lizard" in ancient Greek) was a medium-sized theropod, about 6 m (19.7 ft) long. It may have avoided conflict with its larger, dinosaur-eating relative *Allosaurus* by often preying on water-dwelling animals such as crocodile-like reptiles and turtles.

MORRISONEPPA

Due to their small, fragile bodies, few fossilized insects have been found at the Morrison Formation. *Morrisoneppa* was a flying water bug, around 10 cm (4 in) long. It pierced water-dwelling invertebrates with its tubelike mouthparts, then sucked.

BRACHIOSAURUS

Around 20 m (65.6 ft) long, this sauropodomorph had longer front than back legs, giving its trunk and neck an upright posture. It probably ate leaves on tree branches up to 9 m (30 ft) above the ground.

ALLOSAURUS

Up to 9.7 m (31.8 ft) long, *Allosaurus* was one of the fiercest predators in its habitat, preying on plant-eating dinosaurs including nodosaurs, stegosaurs, and sauropodomorphs. It attacked open-mouthed, slashing at its prey's flesh with its many saw-edged teeth. These teeth were often lost during battles but soon regrew.

GARGOYLEOSAURUS

This dinosaur belonged to the nodosaur group of plant-eaters, which had thick scutes to protect their back and sides from large theropods. When attacked, *Gargoyleosaurus* tried to stay low to the ground to keep its softer underside safe from teeth and claws.

FRUITAFOSSOR

This mammal fed on tiny insects known as termites, which live in groups called colonies. *Fruitafossor* had large, strong front legs that it used to dig into termite nests and to make a safe burrow for itself.

Dicraeosaurus

Dicraeosaurus had long bony spines on its neck, back, and tail, each forming a Y shape. It was these branching spines that earned the dinosaur its name, which means "double-headed lizard" in ancient Greek. Closely related to the diplodocid family (see page 54), *Dicraeosaurus* was a plant-eating sauropodomorph.

STRANGE SPINES

Paleontologists are not certain what *Dicraeosaurus*'s spines were for. The spines may have supported a tall ridge made of muscle, skin, and tough keratin. Such a ridge, particularly if it was bright, might have helped *Dicraeosaurus* recognize other members of its species at mating time. The ridge may have been shown off to possible mates by making twists and turns of the head and neck, as modern flamingos do in their courtship dances.

Alternatively, the spines may not have been covered in a tough sheath, but had their sharp tips exposed to the air. In this case, the spines were probably used to defend the dinosaur against predators. They may have been used in a similar manner to the sharp backward-pointing horns of the modern Arabian oryx, which can stab attacking lions. Whether covered or not, the spines would certainly have prevented tall theropods—such as the local predator *Veterupristisaurus*, which was over 3 m (9.8 ft) tall—from biting down on *Dicraeosaurus*'s vulnerable neck.

NO COMPETITION

Dicraeosaurus had a much shorter neck than its relatives in the diplodocid family. Whereas their necks usually contained 15 bones, called cervical vertebrae, *Dicraeosaurus*'s neck contained only 12 bones, each much shorter. Growing only up to 15 m (49.2 ft) long, *Dicraeosaurus* was also much smaller overall than the diplodocids, which were up to 35 m (115 ft) long. It is likely that *Dicraeosaurus*'s shorter neck and smaller build—although it was still too large for most theropods to attack—gave it some advantages in its habitat.

Dicraeosaurus lived in the region of modern Tanzania, in Africa, alongside several other large plant-eaters. Among these was the immense sauropodomorph *Giraffatitan* (see page 60), which could eat branches 9 m (29.5 ft) high. There was also the smaller, heavy-bodied stegosaur *Kentrosaurus* (see page 46), which fed on low plants up to 1.7 m (5.6 ft) high. *Dicraeosaurus*'s body shape allowed it to feed on leaves between these heights, at up to 3 m (9.8 ft) high, so it did not have to compete for food.

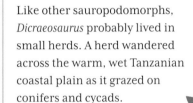

Dicraeosaurus Facts

CLASS	Reptiles
SUPERORDER	Dinosaurs
SUBORDER	Sauropodomorphs
SPECIES	*Dicraeosaurus hansemanni*
RANGE	Africa
TIME PERIOD	155–150 million years ago
SIZE	14–15 m (46–49.2 ft) long

Like other sauropodomorphs, *Dicraeosaurus* probably lived in small herds. A herd wandered across the warm, wet Tanzanian coastal plain as it grazed on conifers and cycads.

Diplodocids

The diplodocids belonged to a group of huge, long-necked plant-eaters known as sauropodomorphs. Diplodocids had extremely long, flexible tails, which they could have cracked like a whip, making a noise louder than a gunshot to startle away predators.

DIPLODOCUS

From the tip of its tail to its snout, *Diplodocus* was up to 32 m (105 ft) long. Like its relatives, *Diplodocus* had slightly shorter front than back legs, making it difficult to raise its long neck very high. *Diplodocus's* neck was probably useful for reaching leaves among thickly growing shrubs and branches, where the dinosaur could not squeeze its immense body.

SUPERSAURUS

Supersaurus (meaning "super lizard" in ancient Greek) was probably the largest member of the diplodocid family, reaching 35 m (115 ft) long and weighing up to 40 tonnes (44 US tons)—more than 20 family cars. A single one of its cervical vertebrae (neck bones) was 1.38 m (4.5 ft) long.

APATOSAURUS

This dinosaur had 15 cervical vertebrae (neck bones), 10 dorsal vertebrae (back bones), 5 sacral vertebrae (hip bones), and around 82 caudal vertebrae (tail bones). The cervical vertebrae contained holes filled with air, making them lighter. *Apatosaurus's* small skull had jaws lined with chisel-like teeth, which could have stripped all the leaves from branches.

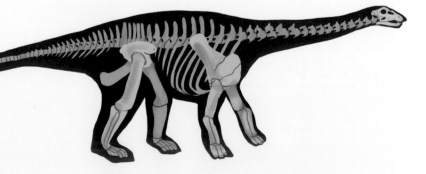

KAATEDOCUS

Like other diplodocids, *Kaatedocus* probably swallowed small stones to help its stomach grind up tough plant material. Scientists call these stones gastroliths ("stomach stones"). Many modern animals, including crocodiles and ostriches, use gastroliths.

Diplodocid Facts

CLASS	Reptiles
SUPERORDER	Dinosaurs
SUBORDER	Sauropodomorphs
RANGE	North America, Europe, Africa, and Asia
TIME PERIOD	170–136 million years ago
SIZE	9–35 m (29.5–115 ft) long

BAROSAURUS

When threatened by an attacker such as *Allosaurus*, *Barosaurus* could rear up on its back legs, using its tail for balance. This action made the dinosaur's chest harder to reach, and when its front legs came crashing down again, *Barosaurus's* weight— over 20 tonnes (22 US tons)— could have been deadly.

BRONTOSAURUS

Brontosaurus lived in a herd, wandering 20 to 40 km (12 to 25 miles) per day across the plains of North America in search of fresh plants. As it walked, *Brontosaurus* may have used its tail to feel the dinosaurs behind and to its sides, so the group could stay together.

Anchiornis

Anchiornis was a birdlike dinosaur, with some features that made it look like a bird—and other features that reveal it was a dinosaur. Today's birds evolved from theropod dinosaurs like *Anchiornis*. The first true birds were flapping their wings by around 72 million years ago.

BECOMING BIRDS

Some of the very earliest theropods may have had a fluffy covering for warmth (see pages 38–39). During the Jurassic Period, some groups of theropods—including compsognathids (see page 59)—started to develop soft, simple feathers. By the Late Jurassic Period, several theropod families had true feathers, with tough, branching stalks. Such feathers are useful for pushing through the air, although most feathered dinosaurs did not use their feathers for flight: They used them for attracting a mate and warming their eggs.

However, by the Late Jurassic Period, some small, feathered theropods had developed other birdlike features: long, feather-covered, winglike arms and a beaklike snout. *Anchiornis* (meaning "near bird" in ancient Greek) was one of these birdlike dinosaurs. It also had long feathers on its back legs, giving it four wings.

Anchiornis represents a stage in the evolution between dinosaurs and birds. Like a dinosaur but unlike a bird, *Anchiornis* had clawed fingers. Birds are toothless, but *Anchiornis* had small teeth in its beak. Paleontologists think that *Anchiornis*'s feathers did not yet have the right blend of strength and flexibility needed for flapping, birdlike flight. However, *Anchiornis* could probably glide short distances by spreading its wings wide and launching itself from a tree branch.

TREE CLIMBER

Anchiornis lived in forests of ginkgo and conifer trees. The curved claws on *Anchiornis*'s toes helped it climb these trees. *Anchiornis* was one of the smallest dinosaurs ever found, just 25 cm (10 in) tall and weighing only 0.25 kg (0.55 lb). On the ground, it was at the mercy of most predators. By climbing into trees, where it could hide among the leaves, it gained a measure of safety.

While sheltering in a tree, *Anchiornis* would have found plenty of crawling insects and spiders to eat. If it waited quietly on a branch, it could also survey the forest floor for small vertebrate prey, including lizards and frogs—then glide down onto them, taking them completely by surprise.

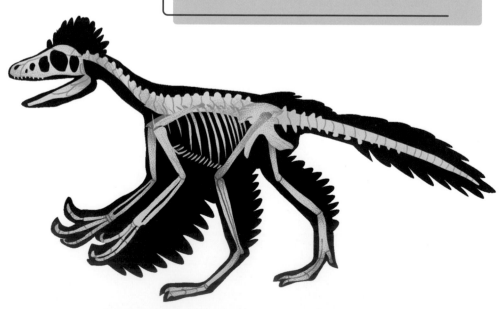

Anchiornis Facts

CLASS	Reptiles
SUPERORDER	Dinosaurs
SUBORDER	Theropods
SPECIES	*Anchiornis huxleyi*
RANGE	China in Asia
TIME PERIOD	163–145 million years ago
SIZE	34–40 cm (13–16 in) long

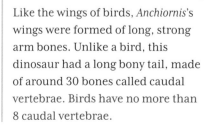

Like the wings of birds, *Anchiornis*'s wings were formed of long, strong arm bones. Unlike a bird, this dinosaur had a long bony tail, made of around 30 bones called caudal vertebrae. Birds have no more than 8 caudal vertebrae.

We know that *Anchiornis* had a red crest and white-and-black wings due to research on a particularly well-preserved fossil. Scientists studied the pigment cells that give feathers their shade, then compared *Anchiornis*'s with those of modern birds.

Solnhofen

The limestone of Germany's Solnhofen region preserved fossils of insects, pterosaurs, and dinosaurs. The most extraordinary find was *Archaeopteryx*, a birdlike dinosaur that gives clues about how dinosaurs evolved into birds.

Around 150 million years ago, Solnhofen lay at the edge of a shallow ocean that was dotted with many small islands. Dead animals that fell or were washed into the water were gently covered by fine-grained mud, in which even their feathers and wings were preserved.

The islands were home to more than 20 species of flying reptiles known as pterosaurs, which plucked fish from the sea and nested on rocks and cliffs. Among the largest pterosaurs here was *Rhamphorhynchus*, with a wingspan of 1.8 m (5.9 ft). *Ctenochasma* was one of the smallest, just 25 cm (10 in) from wingtip to wingtip.

RHAMPHORHYNCHUS

This pterosaur had forward-pointing, needle-like teeth suited to trapping wriggling fish and squid. Its long tail, ending in a vane of tissue and skin, helped steady its flight. *Rhamphorhynchus* snatched prey from the water surface or dived right in, powering through the waves with its broad, flat feet.

ARCHAEOPTERYX

Up to 50 cm (20 in) long, *Archaeopteryx* (meaning "old wing" in ancient Greek) was a theropod dinosaur with features of both dinosaurs and their descendants—birds. Its arms had developed into wings, which were covered in long, strong feathers. It could make short, flapping flights. However, like a dinosaur, it still had teeth in its beak, clawed fingers, and a long bony tail.

PTERODACTYLUS

Like all pterosaurs, *Pterodactylus* (meaning "winged finger") had wings made from skin stretched between its long fourth finger and its legs. It probably showed off its head crest when trying to attract a mate.

CTENOCHASMA

Ctenochasma (meaning "wide comb") was a pterosaur. It had over 400 bristle-like teeth that formed a comb, sticking outward to create a basket-like structure. This was probably used for sieving small fish out of the water using a scooping action.

MESUROPETALA

Mesuropetala was a dragonfly, one of a group of winged insects that is largely unchanged today. Insects were the first animals in the air, around 325 million years ago. Pterosaurs followed 230 million years ago, around 80 million years before birdlike dinosaurs made it off the ground.

COMPSOGNATHUS

Around 1 m (3.3 ft) long, *Compsognathus* was a theropod dinosaur. It may have had short feathers on its body and scales on its back legs and tail. It chased insects and lizards, running fast on its back legs.

Giraffatitan

This dinosaur was one of the largest sauropodomorphs of the Jurassic Period. Its name means "titanic giraffe" in reference to its long neck and immense weight of 40,000 kg (88,200 lb) or more. Until the 1990s, when larger, Cretaceous sauropodomorphs—such as *Argentinosaurus* (see page 82)—were discovered, *Giraffatitan* was believed to be the largest ever land animal.

LIKE A GIRAFFE

Giraffatitan's long front legs made it around 6.8 m (22.3 ft) tall at the shoulder. Its back legs were shorter, giving the dinosaur a slanted rather than horizontal spine—and helping it lift its neck upward. The neck contained 12 or 13 cervical vertebrae (neck bones) and was around 10 m (32.8 ft) long. Like a modern giraffe, *Giraffatitan*'s long legs and neck allowed it to reach high into trees to eat leaves that no other local, ground-dwelling animal could reach.

SMALL BRAIN

This dinosaur's plant-eating diet and lack of predators gave it a slow lifestyle with little need to respond to sudden changes or solve problems. Such a lifestyle does not require a lot of brain power, unlike the lifestyle of a prey-tracking and quick-pouncing theropod. In fact, a large brain would have been a hindrance to *Giraffatitan* because it would have made its head too heavy for its long neck to lift.

Giraffatitan's brain was around the same size as those of other sauropodomorphs, with a volume of about 300 cm³ (18.3 in³). Scientists can make a measure of an animal's intelligence level by comparing its brain size with its body size. *Giraffatitan*'s intelligence level was at the low end for a dinosaur, around 0.62 or 0.79. In comparison, fast-moving birdlike dinosaurs such as *Almas* (see page 84)—which were at the high end of dinosaur intelligence—scored around 5.8.

Giraffatitan Facts

CLASS	Reptiles
SUPERORDER	Dinosaurs
SUBORDER	Sauropodomorphs
SPECIES	*Giraffatitan brancai*
RANGE	Africa
TIME PERIOD	150–145 million years ago
SIZE	23–26 m (75.5–85.3 ft) long

Giraffatitan lived in a region where there were many tall conifer trees, such as cypresses and araucarians. The dinosaur's broad, thick, spoon-shaped teeth sliced off leaves with ease.

Megalosaurs

Megalosaurs (meaning "big lizards" in ancient Greek) were among the largest meat-eaters of the Jurassic Period. They ran on their back legs, grasping prey with their sharp-toothed jaws and clawed hands. They probably also devoured animals they found already dead.

TORVOSAURUS

Torvosaurus had a long, narrow snout with blade-like, curving teeth. Its massive skull was made more lightweight by large openings, known as fenestrae, in front of and behind the eye sockets. The fenestrae behind the eye sockets allowed extra-large, strong jaw muscles to attach to the skull.

DUBREUILLOSAURUS

This dinosaur was named after André Dubreuil, who discovered fossils of its skull and ribs in 1994, in France. During the Jurassic Period, this region was a shallow sea dotted with islands and mangrove swamps. *Dubreuillosaurus* may have caught fish with its three-clawed hands.

AFROVENATOR

Found in northern Africa, this dinosaur was up to 9 m (29.5 ft) long. *Afrovenator* probably preyed on young plant-eating dinosaurs such as the local sauropodomorph *Jobaria*, which reached 18 m (59 ft) long.

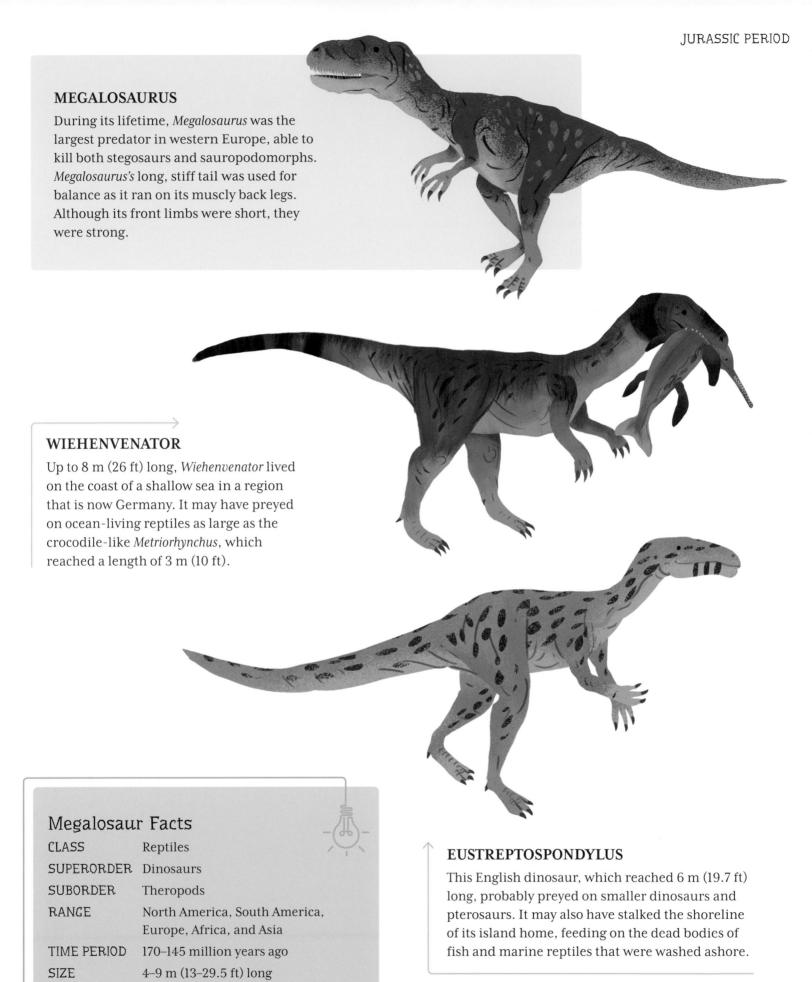

MEGALOSAURUS

During its lifetime, *Megalosaurus* was the largest predator in western Europe, able to kill both stegosaurs and sauropodomorphs. *Megalosaurus's* long, stiff tail was used for balance as it ran on its muscly back legs. Although its front limbs were short, they were strong.

WIEHENVENATOR

Up to 8 m (26 ft) long, *Wiehenvenator* lived on the coast of a shallow sea in a region that is now Germany. It may have preyed on ocean-living reptiles as large as the crocodile-like *Metriorhynchus*, which reached a length of 3 m (10 ft).

Megalosaur Facts

CLASS	Reptiles
SUPERORDER	Dinosaurs
SUBORDER	Theropods
RANGE	North America, South America, Europe, Africa, and Asia
TIME PERIOD	170–145 million years ago
SIZE	4–9 m (13–29.5 ft) long

EUSTREPTOSPONDYLUS

This English dinosaur, which reached 6 m (19.7 ft) long, probably preyed on smaller dinosaurs and pterosaurs. It may also have stalked the shoreline of its island home, feeding on the dead bodies of fish and marine reptiles that were washed ashore.

Yi

The full name of this dinosaur, *Yi qi*, means "wing strange" in Chinese. *Yi* and its close relatives in the Scansoriopterygidae (meaning "climbing wings") family lived in China in the Jurassic Period. These unusual, very small dinosaurs had winglike flaps of skin that let them glide through the air.

STRANGE WINGS

Yi's wings were completely unlike those of birds and other birdlike dinosaurs (see page 56), which were formed of feathers and elongated arm bones. *Yi*'s wings were also unlike the wings of pterosaurs (see page 30), which were formed of flaps of skin and muscle stretching from the back leg to the elongated fourth finger. *Yi*'s wings were made of featherless skin and supported by an extra-long third finger and a long, pointed wristbone that stretched backward from the arm bones.

Yi's wings were a little similar to those of the only truly flying mammals: the bats. However, unlike bats, *Yi* probably could not flap its wings with any strength due to having weak chest and arm muscles. Yet it is probable that *Yi* could glide for short distances, perhaps by opening its arms wide as it launched itself from a tree branch.

LITTLE SNAPPER

Yi was a very small dinosaur, weighing just 380 g (13 oz) and with a wingspan of 60 cm (24 in). Its beaklike snout had small, jutting teeth, which were suited to snapping up insects. It is likely that *Yi* used its gliding ability to snatch flying insects in the thick forest where it lived. Its long hands, as well as curved claws on hands and feet, would have helped it climb trees. Climbing would have allowed *Yi* not only to launch itself into the air but also to hide from predators among the leaves.

Yi and its family had died out by 156 million years ago. No other dinosaurs with similar wings have been found. It is likely that these dinosaurs' lack of speed in the air—as well as their inability to take off from the ground—would have meant they faced increasing competition from predators that were capable of true, flapping flight rather than gliding. By 156 million years ago, local competition included several pterosaurs and birdlike dinosaurs with feathered wings.

Yi Facts

CLASS	Reptiles
SUPERORDER	Dinosaurs
SUBORDER	Theropods
SPECIES	*Yi qi*
RANGE	China in Asia
TIME PERIOD	164–159 million years ago
SIZE	60–70 cm (24–28 in) long

Yi was one of the smallest known theropod dinosaurs. Although its body, legs, and tail were covered by bristly feathers, its wings were featherless.

Cretaceous Period

In the Cretaceous Period (145–66 million years ago), dinosaurs evolved into extraordinary shapes and sizes. This was the time of the fiercest and fastest theropods, the hugest sauropodomorphs, the most heavily protected thyreophorans, and of cerapods with extraordinarily shaped crests, skulls, and neck frills. While some dinosaurs now specialized in eating ants or fish, other were burrowers. As dinosaurs had dominated the land, some reptiles had adapted to life in water. Marine reptiles such as mosasaurs and plesiosaurs were the top predators in the oceans.

The Cretaceous Period ended with one of the greatest catastrophes ever to befall Earth, when an asteroid plunged into the ocean just off the coast of North America. As clouds of dust blocked out the Sun for many months, most animals that weighed over 25 kg (55 lb) died from starvation. The immense size of most reptiles counted against them. The dinosaurs, pterosaurs, and most marine reptiles were wiped out. However, smaller reptiles survived, including snakes, lizards, turtles, and crocodilians. Also among the survivors were some of the dinosaurs that had already evolved into birds, as well as smaller invertebrates, fish, amphibians, and mammals.

Over the course of the Cretaceous Period, the continents continued to separate, moving closer to the positions we know today. The climate was warmer and wetter than now. Sea levels were higher than they are today, so shallow seas covered much of the continents. Flowering plants appeared during the Early Cretaceous Period. These plants produce seeds enclosed in a fruit. Over the course of the Cretaceous Period, flowering plants—including grasses, fruit trees, and daisies—spread across the world. Today, flowering plants make up around 90 percent of all land plants.

Found in Canada around 80–77 million years ago, *Colepiocephale* was a cerapod dinosaur with a strangely dome-shaped skull. Paleontologists think that this feature evolved because it was useful in head-bashing competitions between members of the herd.

Around 70 million years ago in Mongolia, a hungry tyrannosaur, *Tarbosaurus*, surprises two smaller theropods, *Zanabazar* (back) and *Gallimimus* (front), as they drink from a river. With its long legs and slim frame, *Gallimimus* is likely to escape faster than its smaller relative, at up to 56 km/h (35 miles per hour).

Wessex

During the early Cretaceous Period, southern England was drier and warmer than today. The mudstone and sandstone rocks of the region's Wessex Formation have revealed fossils of the fierce theropods and watchful plant-eating dinosaurs that lived around 130 million years ago.

The Wessex Formation underlies today's English county of Dorset and the nearby Isle of Wight. In the Cretaceous Period, there was too little rain here for all but the hardiest trees. This was a shrubland, where low-growing, deep-rooted plants protected their moisture inside hard-coated leaves.

Many of the Wessex Formation fossils were found or studied by 19th-century English paleontologists Mary Ann Mantell, Gideon Mantell, and Richard Owen. Such discoveries led Owen to first use the term dinosaur, meaning "terrible lizard" in ancient Greek.

EOTYRANNUS

An early relative of *Tyrannosaurus*, this theropod (named "dawn tyrant") grew to at least 5 m (16.4 ft) long. It probably preyed on the area's plentiful mammals, grasping with its long, clawed fingers.

HYPSILOPHODON

Just 2 m (6.6 ft) long, *Hypsilophodon* was a lightly built cerapod dinosaur, able to run fast from danger on its two back legs. It cropped plants with its parrot-like beak. The fifth finger on each hand was opposable (could bend to touch the other fingers), helping it to grasp branches and roots.

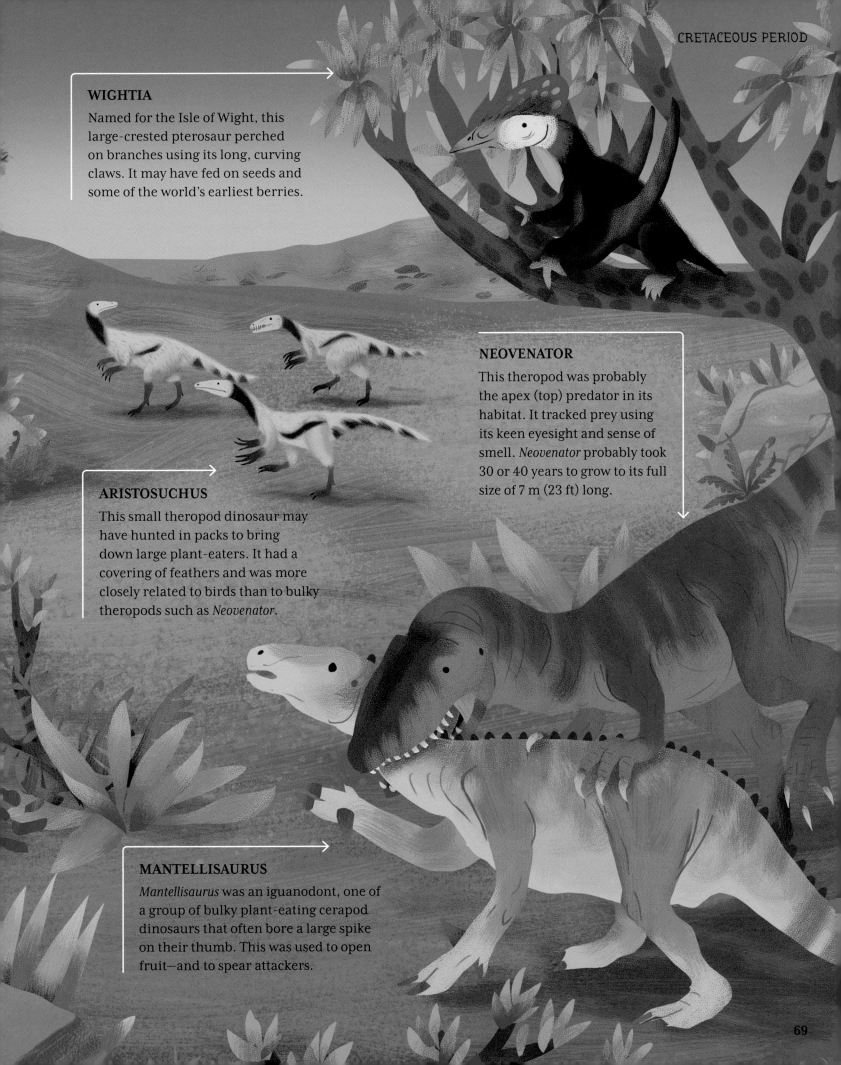

WIGHTIA

Named for the Isle of Wight, this large-crested pterosaur perched on branches using its long, curving claws. It may have fed on seeds and some of the world's earliest berries.

NEOVENATOR

This theropod was probably the apex (top) predator in its habitat. It tracked prey using its keen eyesight and sense of smell. *Neovenator* probably took 30 or 40 years to grow to its full size of 7 m (23 ft) long.

ARISTOSUCHUS

This small theropod dinosaur may have hunted in packs to bring down large plant-eaters. It had a covering of feathers and was more closely related to birds than to bulky theropods such as *Neovenator*.

MANTELLISAURUS

Mantellisaurus was an iguanodont, one of a group of bulky plant-eating cerapod dinosaurs that often bore a large spike on their thumb. This was used to open fruit—and to spear attackers.

69

Baryonyx

This theropod dinosaur had a long crocodile-like snout. Like a modern crocodile, *Baryonyx* spent part of its life in water, where it caught fish; and part on land, where it snatched whichever small- to medium-sized animals it came across.

FISH CATCHER

In 1983, William Walker was exploring a clay pit in southern England. During the week, he worked as a plumber, but he liked to hunt for fossils in his spare time. Walker was lucky: He found a curving claw 31 cm (12 in) long. After the fossil was taken to London's Natural History Museum, it was identified as belonging to a new species of theropod dinosaur, named as *Baryonyx walkeri*. *Baryonyx* means "heavy claw," while *walkeri* credited William Walker.

The claw that Walker found was from the first finger of a *Baryonyx* hand. The dinosaur had three clawed fingers on each hand, but the first claw was the longest. The dinosaur's curving claws were particularly suited to spearing fish. *Baryonyx* had many more teeth than most theropods: 96, compared with *Tyrannosaurus*'s 60. These teeth were pointed and cone-shaped, which made them ideal for gripping and piercing slippery fish.

Baryonyx's long, S-shaped neck and narrow snout were also suited to reaching for fast-moving fish as they darted past. The dinosaur's nostrils were set quite far back on its snout, which is common in air-breathing animals that often dip their faces in water.

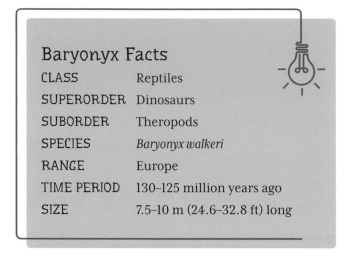

Baryonyx Facts

CLASS	Reptiles
SUPERORDER	Dinosaurs
SUBORDER	Theropods
SPECIES	*Baryonyx walkeri*
RANGE	Europe
TIME PERIOD	130–125 million years ago
SIZE	7.5–10 m (24.6–32.8 ft) long

AVOIDING COMPETITION

Like most animals, *Baryonyx* could probably swim when needed, but its body shape was more suited to wading in shallow water than diving in deep water. *Baryonyx*'s region of England had many shallow lakes and marshes. While other local theropods, such as 7-m (23-ft) *Neovenator*, prowled inland, *Baryonyx* may have stuck to the shore to avoid competition.

Baryonyx's skull had a small, triangular crest above the eyes, which may have formed a feature that helped the dinosaur attract a mate. The tall vertebrae along its back may have formed a ridge or hump.

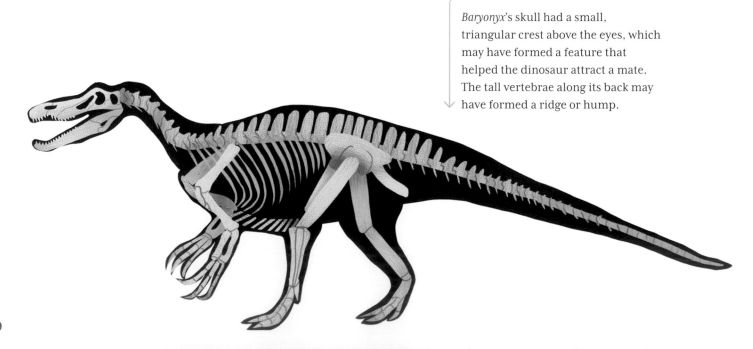

Fish scales have been found in the stomach of a fossilized *Baryonyx*. Some paleontologists think it slapped and hooked fish out of the water using its long claws, like a modern grizzly bear.

Giganotosaurus

One of the largest known theropods, *Giganotosaurus* rivaled its later relative *Tyrannosaurus* in size. Estimates of its length range from 12 m (39.4 ft) to over 13 m (42.7 ft), while it probably weighed between 5,500 kg (12,125 lb) and 8,500 kg (18,740 lb)—more than five family cars.

GIGANTIC JAWS

Giganotosaurus had one of the longest known skulls of any theropod: around 1.6 m (5.2 ft). Its strong, heavily muscled jaws were armed with 76 sharp teeth. The front teeth had up to 12 serrations (small points) per 1 mm (0.04 in) along their front and back edges. Like the serrations on a carving knife, these sliced through scales, flesh, and muscle.

The teeth along the sides of *Giganotosaurus*'s jaws had ridges of enamel (the tough covering of teeth), which helped with mashing. The front tip of *Giganotosaurus*'s lower jaw jutted downward, forming a "chin," which helped to absorb the stress of the blow as this dinosaur bit into prey.

Giganotosaurus chases a young *Andesaurus* that has wandered away from its herd. The theropod's aim was to deliver a slashing bite to its prey, which would soon be weakened by blood loss.

GIANT SOUTHERN LIZARD

With a name meaning "giant southern lizard" in ancient Greek, this dinosaur was the top predator in its South American habitat. Paleontologists believe it preyed on young sauropodomorphs, such as *Andesaurus* and *Limaysaurus*. If *Giganotosaurus* worked with other members of its species, it could have killed fully grown sauropodomorphs.

Paleontologists wonder whether this dinosaur's immense size prevented it from running, but some think it could run at up to 50 km/h (31 miles per hour) on its long back legs—much faster than a sauropodomorph could move. As *Giganotosaurus* ran or walked, its bony, heavy tail balanced the weight of its body and skull. This dinosaur's short arms, with three clawed fingers, may have been used for scratching and piercing prey at close range.

Giganotosaurus Facts

CLASS	Reptiles
SUPERORDER	Dinosaurs
SUBORDER	Theropods
SPECIES	*Giganotosaurus carolinii*
RANGE	Argentina in South America
TIME PERIOD	99–95 million years ago
SIZE	12–13 m (39.4–42.7 ft) long

Western Interior Seaway

The Western Interior Seaway was a sea that split the continent of North America into two during the Late Cretaceous Period. Around 80 million years ago, the ocean's large predators included fearsome sharks and sharp-beaked turtles. The biggest meat-eater of all was the marine reptile *Tylosaurus*.

The seaway was shallow, no more than 760 m (2,495 ft) deep, but 1,000 km (620 miles) wide and 3,200 km (1,990 miles) long. It was sunlit and warm, teeming with life from plants and seaweeds to invertebrates, fish, reptiles, and seabirds. By the end of the Cretaceous, North America's interior had uplifted, and the seaway had dried up.

We have learned about the animals of the seaway through the fossils found in rocks such as the Pierre Shale Formation, which stretches from Canada's Manitoba to the United States' New Mexico. The shale formed on the seafloor as mud was compressed until it hardened.

DOLICHORHYNCHOPS

Dolichorhynchops (meaning "long-nosed face" in ancient Greek) was a plesiosaur, a long-necked marine reptile with four powerful flippers. It had strong jaws and teeth for crushing the shells of small invertebrates.

TYLOSAURUS

Tylosaurus was a mosasaur, a group of marine reptiles that probably evolved from lizards and died out at the end of the Cretaceous. Up to 15.8 m (51.8 ft) long, it could eat most animals in the seaway, from sharks to plesiosaurs.

XIPHACTINUS

Unlike sharks but like most modern fish, this fish had a skeleton made of bone. It grew to more than 5 m (16.4 ft) long, making it 2 m (6.6 ft) longer than the largest bony fish alive today, the ocean sunfish.

ELASMOSAURUS

This plesiosaur had one of the longest necks ever known to exist, up to 7 m (23 ft) long. The reptile had a total length of 10 m (32.8 ft). Its neck may have helped *Elasmosaurus* surprise fish as it lurked in the darker water below—then edged its head upward to bite.

SQUALICORAX

Squalicorax was a shark, a group of fish with skeletons made of bendy cartilage rather than bone. Sharks evolved around 420 million years ago. *Squalicorax* fed on plesiosaurs, fish, and diving pterosaurs.

ARCHELON

The largest turtle ever known to exist, leathery-shelled *Archelon* grew to 4.6 m (15 ft) long. With its sharp, hooked beak, it could pluck hard-shelled prey from the seafloor, as well as give deadly bites to the flesh of fish and reptiles.

Spinosaurus

Reaching more than 14 m (45.9 ft) long, *Spinosaurus* was the longest meat-eating dinosaur ever known to exist. It lived in North Africa, among swamps, lakes, rivers, and seashore mudflats. Like a modern crocodile, it hunted both in water and on land, snatching fish and land-living animals with its long, strong jaws. This dinosaur had a strange sail-shaped structure on its back, formed of bony spines covered with tissue and skin.

SAIL SPECULATION

Spinosaurus's sail was supported by bones known as neural spines, which were extensions of the vertebrae in its backbone. The neural spines grew to 1.65 m (5.4 ft) long. Some paleontologists think that the sail helped the dinosaur to warm up after swimming: The sail's wide surface area would have soaked up plenty of heat from sunshine while the reptile basked.

Other paleontologists think that the sail was shown off to possible mates or that its great height was used to frighten away rival *Spinosauruses* or other theropods. Still other paleontologists think the sail was helpful when catching prey underwater. The modern sailfish has a sail that helps it direct water to drive schools of fish into a tight ball—where they can be snapped up.

SHORE DWELLER

Spinosaurus probably spent much of its time in water as it hunted fish. *Spinosaurus* could swim in pursuit of prey by paddling with its limbs and flicking its tall, paddle-like tail. In the dry season, when pools and swamps dried up, the dinosaur probably caught pterosaurs as they rested—or any medium to small land-living prey it could find. On land, it walked on its back legs. It had wide feet, which may have been webbed, so it did not sink into soft mud.

This dinosaur's long, narrow, crocodile-like snout had cone-shaped teeth. These were suited to pinning and piercing slippery fish. In addition, *Spinosaurus* had three long, clawed fingers—with an extra-long, 50-cm (20-in) claw on its thumb—to grasp prey.

Although *Spinosaurus*'s narrow jaws suggest that it did not prey on large land animals, it could defend itself against local land-living theropods. Fights may have taken place when *Spinosaurus* wandered into theropod hunting grounds during the dry season. One *Spinosaurus* fossil has a bite on its sail made by the 12-m (39.4-ft) long theropod *Carcharodontosaurus*. The bite had healed, so the *Spinosaurus* must have survived the battle.

Spinosaurus Facts

CLASS	Reptiles
SUPERORDER	Dinosaurs
SUBORDER	Theropods
SPECIES	*Spinosaurus aegyptiacus*
RANGE	North Africa
TIME PERIOD	99–93 million years ago
SIZE	12.6–14.3 m (41.3–47 ft) long

Spinosaurus (left) weighed around 7,400 kg (16,300 lb) and was up to 4.4 m (14.4 ft) tall, including its sail. Its vicious adversary *Carcharodontosaurus* weighed around 6,000 kg (13,200 lb) and grew to a height of 3.8 m (12.5 ft).

Pachycephalosaurs

Pachycephalosaurs (meaning "thick-headed lizards" in ancient Greek) had very thick, dome-shaped skulls. These dinosaurs may have used their heads to butt each other, like male mountain goats do today. These dinosaurs were plant-eaters or possibly omnivores.

PACHYCEPHALOSAURUS

The dome of *Pachycephalosaurus's* skull was made of bone up to 25 cm (10 in) thick, which would have cushioned the dinosaur's small brain when headbutting. The dinosaur had a beak for snipping stems, while the sides of the jaw had tiny, leaf-shaped teeth suited to grinding leaves. Yet the beak also bore sharp teeth that could have caught insects.

PRENOCEPHALE

Like their relatives, male *Prenocephales* (meaning "sloping heads") may have had headbutting competitions with rivals, over access to females or the best feeding spots. The winners of these competitions may have become leaders of the herd.

ALASKACEPHALE

This dinosaur was named after the US state of Alaska, where its fossils were first discovered, in an area that was a muddy coastal plain during the Late Cretaceous Period. *Alaskacephale* found plentiful food here, including the leaves of flowering trees, shrubs, herbs, and ferns.

STEGOCERAS

When young, *Stegoceras* may have had a flat skull, which grew into a dome with age. The dome was edged by a shelf ornamented with knobs. An adult *Stegoceras* may have showed off its head to attract a mate, with the largest and most ornamented skulls having most success.

COLEPIOCEPHALE

Like its relatives, *Colepiocephale* (meaning "knuckle head") had large eyes. The region of its brain used for processing smells was unusually big for a dinosaur. Both these features helped *Colepiocephale* sense approaching predators and find food.

Pachycephalosaur Facts

CLASS	Reptiles
SUPERORDER	Dinosaurs
SUBORDER	Cerapods
RANGE	North America and Asia
TIME PERIOD	92–66 million years ago
SIZE	2–4.5 m (6.6–15 ft) long

GOYOCEPHALE

Goyocephale (meaning "decorated head") may have had a flatter skull than most pachycephalosaurs. However, only one skull has yet been found, in the Gobi Desert of Central Asia. It may have belonged to a young *Goyocephale* whose skull was still growing.

Argentinosaurus

This dinosaur was one of the largest known animals that ever walked the Earth, possibly the largest of all. *Argentinosaurus* grew up to 35 m (114.8 ft) long—around the length of seven family cars bumper to bumper. It weighed as much as 75,000 kg (165,000 lb), more than seven times the weight of today's largest land animal, the African bush elephant.

BIGGER AND BETTER

Argentinosaurus was one of the long-necked plant-eaters known as sauropodomorphs. There were two main benefits to *Argentinosaurus*'s immense size. The first was that, as soon as an *Argentinosaurus* was even halfway grown, few theropod dinosaurs would attempt an attack. The second was that an *Argentinosaurus*'s huge abdomen gave room for immensely long, coiled intestines, where nutrients from food are absorbed.

Fossils cannot tell us how long *Argentinosaurus*'s intestines were, but today's largest animal, the 29.9-m (98-ft) blue whale, has intestines more than 200 m (656 ft) long. Food may have spent between one and two weeks in *Argentinosaurus*'s digestive system, allowing the walls of the dinosaur's intestines to soak up maximum energy from its low-energy diet of conifer leaves.

TITANIC TITANOSAURS

Argentinosaurus was a member of the titanosaur group of sauropodomorphs. The titanosaurs lived on all seven continents and were the most common plant-eaters of their time. They were also the last surviving group of sauropodomorphs, becoming extinct after an asteroid hit Earth around 66 million years ago. The titanosaur group includes some of the smallest known sauropodomorphs, such as *Magyarosaurus*, just 6 m (20 ft) long, and the largest, including *Patagotitan*, which may have rivaled *Argentinosaurus* in size.

Female titanosaurs laid eggs in shared nesting grounds, where they dug holes for the eggs with their back feet, then kicked over mud and leaves to hide them. A newly hatched *Argentinosaurus* was only around 1 m (3.3 ft) long and weighed no more than 5 kg (11 lb). It probably received little care from its parents, so its best chance of survival was growing very fast. During its peak growing years, a young *Argentinosaurus* may have gained 40 kg (88 lb) in a day. It still took at least 15 years for an *Argentinosaurus* to grow to full size.

Argentinosaurus Facts

CLASS	Reptiles
SUPERORDER	Dinosaurs
SUBORDER	Sauropodomorphs
SPECIES	*Argentinosaurus huinculensis*
RANGE	Argentina in South America
TIME PERIOD	96–92 million years ago
SIZE	30–35 m (98.4–114.8 ft) long

The largest predator in *Argentinosaurus*'s habitat was the theropod *Mapusaurus*, which grew to 11.5 m (37.7 ft) long. The theropod could not kill a fully grown *Argentinosaurus*, so it may have used the dinosaur like a snack bar, biting off chunks when it could.

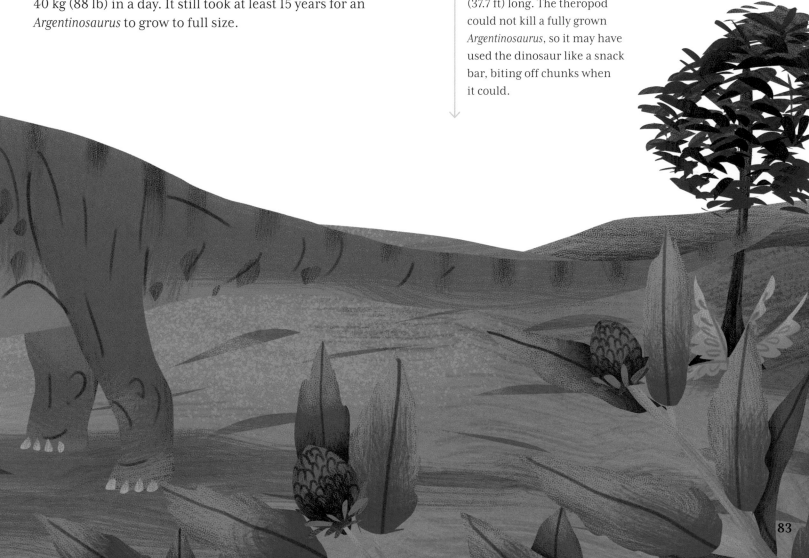

Djadokhta

In Mongolia's Gobi Desert is the Djadokhta Formation of 75-million-year-old sandstone rocks. The formation is rich with fossils of dinosaurs and their eggs. When the rocks formed, this area was dry, sandy, and windblown, just as it is today.

Many of the dinosaurs fossilized at Djadokhta were killed when they were buried in sand by sandstorms or collapsing dunes. The dunes may have collapsed after they became unsteady during sudden heavy rain. Some dinosaurs were trapped while sitting on their nest.

The sand prevented the bodies from being eaten by hungry dinosaurs or birds, although some were nibbled by burrowing invertebrates. The water-soaked sand—and the buried dinosaurs—slowly turned to rock and fossil.

ALMAS

Named after a part-man, part-monster creature in Mongolian stories, this small, birdlike theropod dinosaur preyed on lizards and insects. Females laid their eggs in hollows scraped in the ground, then sat on the eggs to keep them warm. Like *Saurornithoides*, *Almas* was a member of the troodontid group.

HALSZKARAPTOR

Just 60 cm (24 in) long, this dinosaur was a close relative of the small predators *Velociraptor* and *Tsaagan*. While some paleontologists think that *Halszkaraptor* lived only on land, others think it spent time in water, using its jagged-edged beak for catching fish.

PINACOSAURUS

There were no large theropods in this ankylosaur's habitat, but there were small, fast-moving ones. *Pinacosaurus* had a lighter build than most ankylosaurs, giving greater agility. Its moderately sized tail club was heavy enough to send a small theropod flying.

TSAAGAN

Around 2 m (6.6 ft) long, this theropod was built for speed, with long legs and a slim body. It may have hunted in a pack to harass plant-eaters until they tired and weakened.

UDANOCERATOPS

This plant-eater was an early ceratopsian. Unlike its later relative *Triceratops*, it had no horns and only a small neck frill. It is believed that ceratopsians took care of their young until they were big enough to defend themselves.

SAURORNITHOIDES

This birdlike theropod had a longer claw on the second toe of each foot, which it used for pinning down small mammals and reptiles. When running, it lifted this toe off the ground. Quick-thinking *Saurornithoides* had a large brain compared with its body size.

Alvarezsaurids

This family of small, feathered dinosaurs may have been myrmecophagous,
which means they mostly ate termites and ants. Alvarezsaurids had unusually strong
arm and chest muscles, which could have helped them dig into termite
and ant nests with their short arms and hooklike thumb claws.

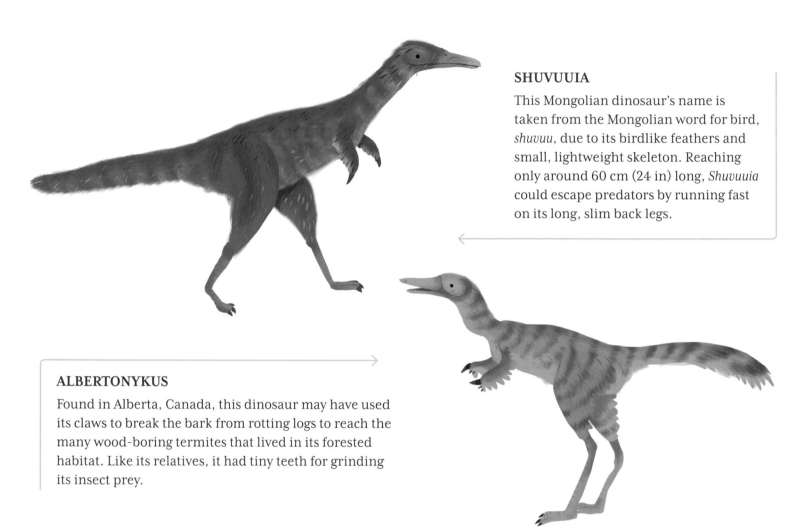

SHUVUUIA

This Mongolian dinosaur's name is
taken from the Mongolian word for bird,
shuvuu, due to its birdlike feathers and
small, lightweight skeleton. Reaching
only around 60 cm (24 in) long, *Shuvuuia*
could escape predators by running fast
on its long, slim back legs.

ALBERTONYKUS

Found in Alberta, Canada, this dinosaur may have used
its claws to break the bark from rotting logs to reach the
many wood-boring termites that lived in its forested
habitat. Like its relatives, it had tiny teeth for grinding
its insect prey.

PARVICURSOR

Like other members of its family,
Parvicursor had one large, clawed
finger on each hand, as well as
two additional fingers too tiny to
be functional. The main, hooklike
finger was suited to breaking open
termite nests. *Parvicursor's* long
snout was ideal for reaching into
nests, a little like the snout of a
modern anteater.

ALVAREZSAURUS

Alvarezsaurus was the first dinosaur in its family to be discovered, in Argentina in 1991. It was named after the Argentinian historian Gregorio Álvarez. At first, *Alvarezsaurus* was thought to be a flightless bird, but it is now thought to be part of the coelurosaur group of feathered theropod dinosaurs from which birds evolved.

LINHENYKUS

Named after the city of Linhe in China, this small alvarezsaurid probably weighed as much as a large parrot. It may have had a long tongue that, like the tongue of a modern woodpecker, helped it reach hiding termites.

Alvarezsaurid Facts

CLASS	Reptiles
SUPERORDER	Dinosaurs
SUBORDER	Theropods
RANGE	North America, South America, and Asia
TIME PERIOD	97–66 million years ago
SIZE	0.4–2 m (1.3–6.6 ft) long

QIUPANYKUS

In 2018, fossils of this dinosaur were found with the broken eggs of oviraptorid dinosaurs. This has made paleontologists wonder if *Qiupanykus*—and perhaps its relatives— sometimes used its hooked claws to break into eggs to eat.

Parasaurolophus

Parasaurolophus (meaning "near crested lizard" in ancient Greek) was named for its tall head crest. Paleontologists have suggested many different purposes for this crest, from attracting a mate to making loud calls. The crest may have been bigger in adult males than in young males and females.

PERFECT PLANT-EATER

Parasaurolophus belonged to the cerapod suborder of dinosaurs. These dinosaurs were plant-eaters with horny, sharp-edged, beaklike jaws for snipping off twigs. *Parasaurolophus* was in the hadrosaur family of cerapods, which are often called duckbilled dinosaurs due to their flattened snout that resembled a duck's beak.

A hadrosaur's beak was toothless, but at the back of its jaws were several rows of grinding teeth that easily chewed tough plant material. A hadrosaur also had muscly cheeks that helped it hold lots of food in its mouth. These advantages allowed hadrosaurs to eat and digest large amounts of leaves, twigs, and pine needles—and also helped them become the most common plant-eating dinosaurs of the Late Cretaceous Period. One member of the family, *Edmontosaurus* (see page 102), was one of the last surviving dinosaurs.

Parasaurolophus could walk on either two or four legs. When wandering slowly from plant to plant, it probably balanced its great weight—of up to 5,000 kg (11,000 lb)—on all four legs. Yet when it was threatened by a theropod dinosaur, *Parasaurolophus* could run fast on its long back legs.

CURIOUS CREST

Many paleontologists think that *Parasaurolophus*'s head crest helped it communicate. The long, curving crest was hollow. When *Parasaurolophus* called to its herd, the sounds bounced around inside the crest, which made them louder. In the same way, the hollow body of a guitar makes the sound of a plucked string louder.

Another possible use for the crest was to cool *Parasaurolophus* down when it got hot. The crest had a large surface area, which allowed lots of body heat to escape. An adult male *Parasaurolophus* may also have shown off his large crest at mating time, with larger-crested males having more success with females.

Parasaurolophus's hollow crest was formed by extended premaxilla and nasal bones. In other dinosaurs, the premaxilla bones are small bones at the tip of the upper jaw. The nasal bones usually form the top of the snout.

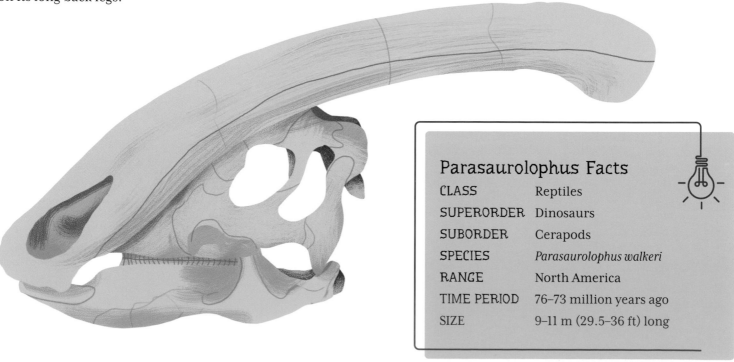

Parasaurolophus Facts

CLASS	Reptiles
SUPERORDER	Dinosaurs
SUBORDER	Cerapods
SPECIES	*Parasaurolophus walkeri*
RANGE	North America
TIME PERIOD	76–73 million years ago
SIZE	9–11 m (29.5–36 ft) long

Like a modern deer, *Parasaurolophus* may have lived in a large herd, ranging from several hundred during the mating season to a dozen or less at other times. A range of calls helped the herd stay together and keep safe from predators.

Saltasaurids

These sauropodomorphs were long-necked, long-tailed plant-eaters.
Most saltasaurids were around 15 m (49 ft) long, making them smaller than the majority
of Late Cretaceous sauropodomorphs. Yet saltasaurids had the added protection
of bony scutes along their back.

SALTASAURUS

This dinosaur was named after
Salta, the region of Argentina
where it was first found. Its back
and sides were protected by oval
scutes 12 cm (5 in) wide, with
many smaller scutes filling the
gaps between. The scutes gave
protection from the teeth and
claws of huge theropods such
as *Carnotaurus*.

NEUQUENSAURUS

One of the smallest known saltasaurids,
Neuquensaurus grew to around 8 m (26 ft long)
and a weight of 10 tonnes (11 US tons). Its thick
legs and stump-like feet (it did not have any toes
or claws on its front feet) were suited to slow
walking rather than running.

ALAMOSAURUS

Alamosaurus grew to 34 m (112 ft) long,
making it by far the largest saltasaurid
and the biggest dinosaur found in North
America. *Alamosaurus* was also one of
the latest surviving sauropodomorphs,
becoming extinct after an asteroid hit Earth
66 million years ago.

BONATITAN

Like other saltasaurids, *Bonatitan* probably lived in a herd, which offered particular protection to younger and weaker members of the group. Females may have laid their eggs in group nesting grounds, where they all dug holes for their eggs before covering them with soil.

Saltasaurid Facts

CLASS	Reptiles
SUPERORDER	Dinosaurs
SUBORDER	Sauropodomorphs
RANGE	North America, South America, Europe, and Asia
TIME PERIOD	85.8–66 million years ago
SIZE	8–34 m (26–112 ft) long

OPISTHOCOELICAUDIA

Opisthocoelicaudia (meaning "back cavity tail" in ancient Greek) had tail bones with backs that curved inward and fronts that curved outward, so they slotted together to make the tail unusually flexible. The dinosaur may have reared up on its back legs to reach into trees, using its tail for balance.

ROCASAURUS

Rocasaurus fed on leaves and buds, stripping them from branches with its blunt, peg-shaped teeth. Like a modern cow, the dinosaur probably kept plant material in its stomach for a long time as it was slowly broken down by tiny living things, called bacteria, that made their home there.

91

Oryctodromeus

Oryctodromeus (meaning "burrowing runner" in ancient Greek) was one of the few dinosaurs known to dig burrows. It was a small, plant-eating dinosaur that could run from danger on its back legs. *Oryctodromeus* was a relative of plant-eaters including the ceratopsians and pachycephalosaurs.

A burrow offers safety from predators, as well as shelter from extremes of weather—from hot summer days to stormy winter nights.

BURROWING FOR BABIES

In 2007, the fossils of an adult *Oryctodromeus* and two of its young were discovered in an underground burrow. The burrow was around 2 m (6.6 ft) long and 0.7 m (2.3 ft) wide, just the right size to house the adult with her young lying close to her. The entrance tunnel had kinks in it, which prevented easy entrance by predators.

The burrow was similar to those of modern mammals such as hyenas and rabbits. Like those animals, *Oryctodromeus* probably dug a burrow to make a safe place to raise its young. The fairly large size of the young in the dinosaur's burrow—around 1.3 m (4.3 ft) long—suggests that *Orcytodromeus* looked after its babies for many months. Since an *Oryctodromeus* was neither an immense size nor covered by bony plates, a long period of care by a parent—in the safety of a burrow—was an excellent way to ensure the survival of the species.

BUILT FOR DIGGING

Burrowing animals such as today's moles, which spend most of their time underground, have very short, powerful front limbs with large paws adapted for digging. In contrast, *Oryctodromeus* had front limbs as suited to digging as those of modern animals, such as hyenas and rabbits, that spend some of their time burrowing—and the rest of it running fast above ground.

Oryctodromeus had strong, muscly shoulders and arms for digging, but its hands were not as spade-like as a mole's. Since *Oryctodromeus* ran only on its back legs, its short, broad front limbs had no effect on its speed. The dinosaur's hips were sturdy, which would have helped it kick mud out of the burrow. Its hips were also narrow, which reduced the necessary width of the burrow. *Oryctodromeus*'s snout ended in a particularly broad horny beak, which may have also been useful for burrowing.

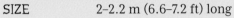

Oryctodromeus Facts

CLASS	Reptiles
SUPERORDER	Dinosaurs
SUBORDER	Cerapods
SPECIES	*Oryctodromeus cubicularis*
RANGE	North America
TIME PERIOD	95 million years ago
SIZE	2–2.2 m (6.6–7.2 ft) long

Hell Creek

Hundreds of fossils have been found in the rocks around Hell Creek, which is today in Montana, in the United States. The fossils date from the end of the Cretaceous Period, around 67 to 66 million years ago.

In the Late Cretaceous Period, Hell Creek lay on the shore of the Western Interior Seaway, a large sea that split North America in two. The area was a plain, an expanse of flat land, where streams and rivers wound their way to the ocean. The climate was warm and wet, giving life to a vast forest where both flowering trees and conifers grew tall.

The fossils at Hell Creek belong to both land- and water-living animals. There were reptiles such as dinosaurs, pterosaurs, crocodilians, lizards, snakes, and turtles. They lived alongside birds, insects, fish, frogs, and mammals.

DAKOTARAPTOR

This feathered hunter was a dromaeosaurid, a member of a group of dinosaurs with a narrow snout and long tail. Like other dromaeosaurids, *Dakotaraptor's* second toes had an extra-long claw, which was held off the ground while running—and was used for pinning and slashing prey.

STRUTHIOMIMUS

This ostrich-like dinosaur fled from predators on its long back legs, possibly reaching a speed of 50 to 80 km/h (31 to 50 miles per hour). It hooked branches using its long fingers, then cropped buds and shoots with its long, toothless beak.

AVISAURUS

Avisaurus was an early bird. Unlike modern birds, it had teeth in its beak, as well as clawed fingers. It flew over Hell Creek on the lookout for insects, lizards, and small mammals, but it may also have eaten seeds and shoots.

TOROSAURUS

Like most ceratopsians, *Torosaurus* had horns and a neck frill. Its skull grew up to 2.77 m (9.1 ft) long, making it one of the largest known skulls of any land animal. When full size, *Torosaurus* could weigh 12,000 kg (26,500 lb), as much as 150 adult men.

CIMOLOMYS

Cimolomys was a small, ratlike mammal. Like modern mammals, its skin was covered in hair. It had long, broad front teeth suited to cracking seeds, as well as notched teeth in its cheeks that were ideal for chewing tough roots.

CHAMPSOSAURUS

This crocodile-like reptile lived in the rivers and lakes of Hell Creek. Like modern crocodiles, it had a long, narrow snout. Its strong jaw muscles and many sharp teeth allowed it to catch wriggling, slippery fish.

Therizinosaurus

This dinosaur was a theropod, but unlike most other theropods, it was a plant-eater. *Therizinosaurus* belonged to a group of theropods known as maniraptorans (meaning "hand snatchers" in Latin). Maniraptorans were often feathered and usually had long arms and three-fingered hands. Other maniraptorans include alvarezsaurids, oviraptorids—and birds.

STANDING TALL

Therizinosaurus was the largest known maniraptoran, growing to a height of 5 m (16.4 ft). This dinosaur had the benefit of being taller than most other plant-eaters—and all of the predators—in its habitat, which lay in the region of modern Mongolia. The tallest local predator was 3.5-m (11.5-ft) tall *Tarbosaurus* (see page 67), which could not have reached *Therizinosaurus*'s vulnerable neck when the plant-eater stood up straight on its back legs.

REACHING HIGH

Therizinosaurus's name means "cutting lizard" in ancient Greek. This refers to the three huge claws on each of its hands, which were unusually straight and stiff. These claws grew to 1 m (3.3 ft) long, making them the longest of any known animal.

Although such claws might have been useful when attacked by a theropod, paleontologists think the main use of this dinosaur's long claws, fingers, and arms—which grew to an immense 2.4 m (7.9 ft) long—was to hook down high tree branches. This ability meant that *Therizinosaurus* could reach higher leaves than local sauropodomorphs, so it did not need to compete for food. Its long, flexible neck also helped it feed high up with little effort.

Therizinosaurus fed in a manner similar to a ground sloth (see page 117), which also hooked branches with its claws. This is an example of convergent evolution, when two animals develop similar features not because they are closely related but in response to the same problem—in this case, how a heavy, land-based animal can feed on high leaves.

Therizinosaurus Facts

CLASS	Reptiles
SUPERORDER	Dinosaurs
SUBORDER	Theropods
SPECIES	*Therizinosaurus cheloniformis*
RANGE	Mongolia in Asia
TIME PERIOD	70 million years ago
SIZE	9–10 m (29.5–32.8 ft) long

Unlike most theropods, which had three main toes, *Therizinosaurus* had four main toes on each of its back legs (as well as a fifth short toe that did not touch the ground). Its main toes were strong and broad, so they could take the full weight of this heavy dinosaur, which reached 5,000 kg (11,000 lb).

Ceratopsians

These plant-eaters take their name from the ancient Greek words for "horned faces."
Later ceratopsians had large horns, as well as frills that covered their necks.
These were probably features that helped attract a mate. All ceratopsians
had a strong beak for snapping twigs and leaves.

PENTACERATOPS

Pentaceratops (meaning "five-horned face")
had a nose horn, two brow horns, and two
horns on its cheeks. It also had triangular
hornlets on its frill. It used its sharp-
edged, toothless beak to snip branches
from ferns, conifers, and cycads. It chewed
this tough material with hundreds of rows
of closely packed, leaf-shaped teeth.

PROTOCERATOPS

Protoceratops (meaning "first horned face") was
an early ceratopsian that lived 75 to 72 million
years ago. It had a large neck frill made of bone
with skin-covered holes that made it lighter.
Although *Protoceratops* had no horns, it had a
bony bump above its nostrils.

GRACILICERATOPS

This early ceratopsian lived from
96 to 89 million years ago. It was
smaller than its later relatives, only
around 2 m (6.6 ft) long. Unlike heavier,
later ceratopsians, it walked on two
legs. *Graciliceratops* (meaning "graceful
horned face") had a small frill that
jutted from the back of its skull.

TRICERATOPS

Triceratops (meaning "three-horned face") grew up to 9 m (29.5 ft) long, while its brow horns were around 1 m (3.3 ft) long. Unlike other ceratopsians, *Triceratops* had a solid frill without skin-covered holes. *Triceratops* lived from 68 to 66 million years ago, when it was wiped out along with all the other dinosaurs, apart from birds.

KOSMOCERATOPS

This dinosaur had the most ornamented skull of any known dinosaur, with five horns on its face and ten curved hornlets on its frill. *Kosmoceratops* bones were first discovered in 2006, in Utah, USA. It had five toes on its front feet and four toes on its back feet.

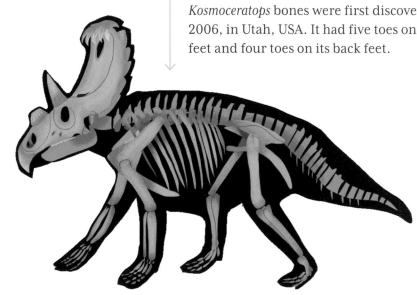

DIABLOCERATOPS

As well as the horns above its eyes, *Diabloceratops* had two long spikes on its neck frill. These features probably helped *Diabloceratops* to recognize other members of its species. At mating time, dinosaurs with the sturdiest frill and horns probably won the most mates, as male deer with big antlers do today.

Ceratopsian Facts

CLASS	Reptiles
SUPERORDER	Dinosaurs
SUBORDER	Cerapods
RANGE	North America, Europe, and Asia
TIME PERIOD	161–66 million years ago
SIZE	1–9 m (3.3–30 ft) long

Velociraptor

Velociraptor was a small, fast-moving meat-eater. It was a member of the dromaeosaurid group of feathered theropod dinosaurs. *Velociraptor* chased small prey such as lizards and mammals, but was also quick-thinking enough to attack a weakened dinosaur when it saw one.

CATCH AND CLAW

Velociraptor means "swift snatcher" in Latin. With its lightweight build, this dinosaur could run fast on its long back legs, reaching 40 km/h (28 miles per hour) for short bursts. It had an extra-long, curved claw on the second toe of each foot, which it held off the ground as it ran. This claw measured 6.5 cm (2.6 in) around its outer edge.

When it caught up with prey, *Velociraptor* leaped on top, pinning down the animal with its claws. This method is used by modern birds of prey such as eagles. Then *Velociraptor* may have torn flesh from its living victim until the unlucky animal died from blood loss or shock. *Velociraptor* had around 30 teeth, which were small and curved with jagged edges that helped it slice flesh. It had a long, narrow snout that was suited to feeding on small animals—or ripping at larger ones.

FIGHTING DINOSAURS

In 1971, a fossil was discovered of a fighting *Velociraptor* and *Protoceratops*, which grew to around 2.5 m (8.2 ft) long. Since *Protoceratops* was much more sturdily built than *Velociraptor*, this fossil tells us this *Velociraptor* might have been extremely fearless, perhaps because it was desperately hungry or because it was young and inexperienced. Alternatively, this *Velociraptor* may have noticed that the *Protoceratops* was old, sick, or injured.

The two animals were locked in combat when they were buried by a sandstorm or sand dune collapse in the desert where they lived. The *Velociraptor* was underneath its prey, with one of its extra-long claws stuck in the *Protoceratops*'s throat. The *Protoceratops* was biting the right arm of its attacker with its hard beak. If the *Velociraptor* had managed to pierce its victim's windpipe, or one of the major blood vessels in its throat, it would have won this battle.

Velociraptor Facts

CLASS	Reptiles
SUPERORDER	Dinosaurs
SUBORDER	Theropods
SPECIES	*Velociraptor mongoliensis*
RANGE	Asia
TIME PERIOD	75–71 million years ago
SIZE	1.5–2 m (4.9–6.6 ft) long

Velociraptor (right) and *Protoceratops* lived in Asia in a dry, sandy habitat. Hardy, low-growing shrubs provided food for plant-eaters.

Frenchman

Along Canada's Frenchman River is a rock formation that has revealed fossils of some of the last dinosaur species, which were alive when an asteroid struck Earth around 66 million years ago. The rocks also hold a layer of dust that settled in the aftermath of this deadly impact.

When a 10-km (6-mile) wide asteroid plunged into the ocean just off the coast of Mexico, tall waves swamped the land and the intense heat set off wildfires. The impact sent clouds of dust into the air, blocking sunlight for up to a year. Without sunlight, plants died, followed by many plant-eaters—and finally the meat-eaters that fed on them.

All the dinosaurs and pterosaurs died. Around three-quarters of other animals died along with them. Most survivors were small animals, which needed less food, and were flexible about what they ate, making do with dead animals, insects, and nuts until the dust cleared and fallen seeds grew into new plants.

EDMONTOSAURUS
A relative of *Parasaurolophus*, this plant-eating dinosaur lived in a herd, making calls to its family as it grazed. It grew to 13 m (42.7 ft) long. Within months of the asteroid strike, every *Edmontosaurus* was dead.

ALPHADON
Just 30 cm (12 in) long, this mammal was an omnivore, finding fruit, seeds, and invertebrates using its keen eyesight, sense of smell, and sensitive whiskers. Like other small mammals, it probably survived the catastrophe.

CIMOLOPTERYX

Survivors of the disaster included some of the dinosaurs that had evolved into birds. Small, toothless birds such as *Cimolopteryx* could use their hard beak to crack long-lasting, tough food such as nuts and seeds.

SPHAEROTHOLUS

This dome-headed pachycephalosaur dinosaur lived in North America from 73 to 66 million years ago. Although it ate both leaves and small animals, it fell victim to hunger and desperate predators after the asteroid impact.

THESCELOSAURUS

When the asteroid struck, *Thescelosaurus* (meaning "wondrous lizard" in ancient Greek) was one of the most common plant-eaters in North America. It fed on low plants, which it chewed with the help of its muscly cheeks.

OPISTHOTRITON

Opisthotriton belonged to a group of amphibians known as salamanders, which are alive today. It ate water-dwelling invertebrates—and survived up until 64 million years ago.

Oviraptorids

Found only in Asia, these feathered theropod dinosaurs had toothless, sharp-edged beaks. These were used for clipping leaves, as well as for cracking seeds and nuts, as most parrots do today. Some oviraptorids may also have snapped up lizards and insects.

OVIRAPTOR

This dinosaur, along with its family, takes its name from the ancient Greek words for "egg snatcher." It was named in 1924, after an *Oviraptor* fossil was found on a nest of eggs thought to belong to *Protoceratops*, suggesting that it died while stealing them. Further study revealed that the eggs belonged to the *Oviraptor*, which was warming them as most birds do today.

JIANGXISAURUS

Found in China's Jiangxi Province, this dinosaur had three, clawed fingers on each hand, which could have grabbed branches, fruit, or even beetles. *Jiangxisaurus's* arms—too short and weak to be true wings—bore long feathers that were useful for warming nests of eggs.

KHAAN

Differences in the tail bones of male and female *Khaans* suggest that males had a large fan of tail feathers, while females did not. Like a modern peacock, male *Khaans* may have shown off their tail fan to attract a mate.

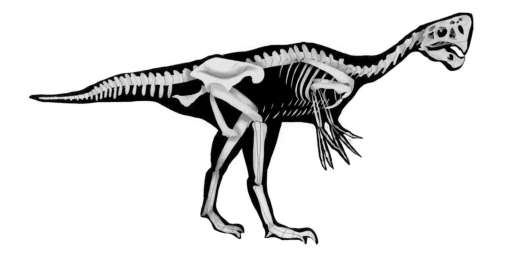

CITIPATI

Up to 2.9 m (9.5 ft) long, *Citipati* had a crest formed by enlarged bones in its upper jaw and nose. The crest and other skull bones had many air-filled holes, allowing sounds to reverberate inside. This may have helped *Citipati* make loud calls to its herd.

BANJI

Named for the Chinese words for "striped crest," *Banji* had ridges on its crest. This decorative feature may have helped attract a mate. Only one fossil of *Banji* has been found, in China's Guangdong Province. It belonged to a young dinosaur that had grown only 65 cm (26 in) long.

Oviraptorid Facts

CLASS	Reptiles
SUPERORDER	Dinosaurs
SUBORDER	Theropods
RANGE	Asia
TIME PERIOD	84–66 million years ago
SIZE	0.5–2.9 m (1.6–9.5 ft) long

OKSOKO

Oksoko was named after a triple-headed eagle that appears in myths told in central and northern Asia. The first discovery of *Oksoko* fossils was of a group that died together, perhaps in a flash flood or landslide. Three of the group's skulls had been preserved.

105

Tyrannosaurus

Tyrannosaurus (meaning "tyrant lizard") was one of the largest meat-eaters that ever walked the Earth. Although theropods such as Spinosaurus were slightly longer, Tyrannosaurus had a stronger bite than any other dinosaur—more than 100 times more powerful than a human's jaws.

BUILT FOR KILLING

Tyrannosaurus had 60 curving teeth up to 30.5 cm (12 in) long. Each sharp tooth had jagged edges that helped *Tyrannosaurus* carve through scales, skin, muscles, and bones. The dinosaur's skull was up to 1.5 m (5 ft) long, with exceptionally thick, strong jaw bones that were snapped closed by powerful muscles.

Although *Tyrannosaurus* had short arms, they were muscled enough to hold on to struggling prey while the dinosaur inflicted a deep and deadly wound with its jaws. *Tyrannosaurus* had only two fingers, but each was armed with a long, sharp claw.

This dinosaur's eyes were forward-facing, which helped the two eyes work together to judge the distance and speed of fast-fleeing prey. In contrast, many plant-eating dinosaurs had eyes on the sides of their head to watch all around for predators. The shape of *Tyrannosaurus*'s skull suggests that a large portion of its brain was dedicated to analyzing smells, which helped it detect prey more than 1,000 m (3,280 ft) away.

Overall, *Tyrannosaurus* had a relatively large brain compared with its body size, giving it around the same intelligence level as a modern bird. This meant that *Tyrannosaurus* could think quickly, respond fast to changing situations, and even plan ahead the best way to corner its unlucky prey.

TOP HUNTER

Like today's large meat-eaters, such as lions and wolves, *Tyrannosaurus* probably hunted live prey as well as feeding on dead animals it found, which is known as scavenging. At 4 m (13.1 ft) tall, this dinosaur's size and strength made it an apex predator, with no predators of its own unless it was young or sick. *Tyrannosaurus* could take its pick of plant-eating dinosaurs as big as 9-m- (29.5-ft-) long *Triceratops* and 8-m- (26.2-ft-) long *Ankylosaurus*. Like lions and wolves, *Tyrannosaurus* may have hunted in a pack to bring down the largest prey of all: sauropodomorphs such as *Alamosaurus*.

Tyrannosaurus Facts

CLASS	Reptiles
SUPERORDER	Dinosaurs
SUBORDER	Theropods
SPECIES	*Tyrannosaurus rex*
RANGE	North America
TIME PERIOD	68–66 million years ago
SIZE	11–13 m (36–42.7 ft) long

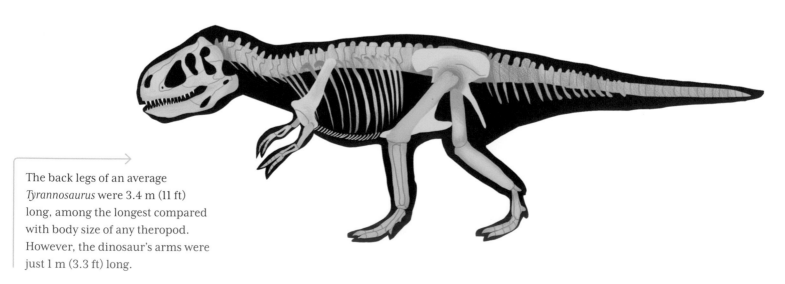

The back legs of an average *Tyrannosaurus* were 3.4 m (11 ft) long, among the longest compared with body size of any theropod. However, the dinosaur's arms were just 1 m (3.3 ft) long.

Tyrannosaurus bite marks have been found on *Triceratops* fossils. The marks suggest that *Tyrannosaurus* often tried to rip off the plant-eater's neck frill to reach its soft neck.

After the Dinosaurs

The time since the last dinosaurs died—the last 66 million years—
is often called the Age of Mammals. Whereas reptiles dominated the Triassic,
Jurassic, and Cretaceous Periods, it has been the turn of mammals ever since.
While the hungry dinosaurs were alive, most mammals were small.
Over the next few million years, mammals grew larger and adapted to new
habitats and lifestyles. Like reptiles before them, some mammals even adapted
to living in water. The first fully ocean-dwelling mammals evolved around
50 million years ago. In fact, it is a marine mammal—the blue whale—
that holds the record for being the largest animal that ever lived, at
29.9 m (98 ft) long and weighing up to 199,000 kg (439,000 lb).

The Age of Mammals has also been a successful time for birds, the closest living
relatives of dinosaurs. Birds evolved from some of the smallest dinosaurs, but after
the extinction of their large relatives, some birds grew very big and fierce.
Like mammals, birds moved into new habitats, a few even losing the ability to fly
and becoming fast runners or swimmers instead.

The smartest animals ever to walk the Earth are mammals: humans.
Along with apes and monkeys, humans belong to a group of large-brained mammals
known as primates, which evolved in rain forests at around the time that the
dinosaurs became extinct. The arrival of modern humans, around 300,000 years ago,
was disastrous for the world's largest animals—from mammoths to crocodilomorphs—
because they were hunted to extinction by a new top predator. A new wave of
extinctions began, the first caused by a single species. The extinctions of animals from
frogs to birds continues today, due to careless human activities such as burning fuels,
cutting down trees, and dropping waste. Yet humans are also the first animal species
that loves to learn about and care for other animals. This smart species can make sure
that the current wave of extinctions is not as devastating as the last.

Up to 1.9 m (6.2 ft) tall,
Titanis was a fast-running,
flightless bird. It was one
of North America's largest
predators 5–1.8 million
years ago.

Around 13 million years ago, the rain forests of South America teemed with mammals such as the monkey *Cebupithecia* and the glyptodont *Boreostemma*. Protected by bony scutes, *Boreostemma* was about 2 m (6.6 ft) long and ate plants. Both these mammal species have been extinct for millions of years, but the cane toad, an amphibian, has survived to the present.

Riversleigh

The fossils of about 300 species of extinct animals have been found at northern Australia's Riversleigh site. Around 20 million years ago, this area was a rain forest where strange marsupial mammals hid and hunted.

Marsupials are a group of mammals that give birth to tiny, undeveloped young, which mothers carry in a pouch on their abdomen. In contrast, most mammals are placentals, which give birth to well-developed young—a safer method for babies but less safe for mothers.

Marsupials evolved in the Americas, around 90 million years ago. By about 50 million years ago, marsupials had reached Australia over land bridges. They began to adapt to many habitats and lifestyles. Today, most Australian mammals are marsupials, as they were 20 million years ago. Marsupials are also found in the Americas as well as New Guinea and surrounding islands.

NIMIOKOALA

Around 30 cm (12 in) long, this koala was about one-third the size of the modern koala. It ate the leaves of rain forest trees, and became extinct when the climate grew drier and this region changed from forest to scrub.

BALBAROO FANGAROO

This extinct kangaroo had long upper canine (front side) teeth, forming fangs. Since *Balbaroo* was a plant-eater, the fangs may only have been used by males when fighting over females. Unlike modern kangaroos, *Balbaroo* scurried rather than hopped.

NIMBADON

This marsupial ate stems and leaves, climbing rain forest trees with the help of its sharp claws, which it retracted (pulled back) when walking. It lived in a family group.

LEKANELEO

Often called a marsupial lion, although it was not related to cats, this predator had long, pointed teeth. Its agile body was suited to climbing trees to pursue prey or to ambush floor-dwelling prey from a branch.

NIMBACINUS

This sharp-toothed, strong-jawed predator, just 50 cm (20 in) long, ate small birds, mammals, and reptiles. *Nimbacinus* and its relatives were the rain forest's most common predators.

WONAMBI

Up to 6 m (19.7 ft) long, this snake lay in wait for passing animals, then coiled itself quickly around them. It squeezed until the prey's heart stopped beating. Snakes evolved from lizards around 94 million years ago.

Paraceratherium

Paraceratherium was one of the largest land mammals of all time. It grew to around 4.8 m (15.7 ft) tall and 7.4 m (24.3 ft) long. It may have weighed up to 20,000 kg (44,000 lb), double the weight of the largest African bush elephants, which are today's largest land mammals. *Paraceratherium* (meaning "near hornless beast") was a hornless rhinoceros.

RHINO RELATIVE

Paraceratherium was a relative of today's rhinoceroses. Like them, it was a member of the Perissodactyl order of mammals. Also known as odd-toed ungulates, animals in this order are usually hoofed mammals (ungulates) with an odd number of weight-carrying toes on each foot, either three (for rhinos and tapirs) or one (for horses).

Like its modern relatives, *Paraceratherium* was a plant-eater. The bones of its snout suggest that it either had a long, flexible upper lip or it had a short trunk, like an elephant's but much shorter. *Paraceratherium* used its grasping lip or trunk to grab leaves from shrubs and trees. With the dinosaurs long gone, *Paraceratherium*'s great size—combined with its long neck—allowed it to reach branches that other plant-eaters could not. In contrast, modern rhinos are 1.8 m (5.9 ft) tall, and eat grasses and other low plants.

HORNS OR TUSKS

Unlike a modern rhinoceros, *Paraceratherium* did not have horns. A modern rhino's horns grow from the top of its snout and are made of keratin, the same material found in hair, hooves, and beaks. However, *Paraceratherium* did have tusk-like front teeth called incisors.

Paraceratherium may have used its tusks for levering, bending, and breaking branches. It is also possible that the tusks were useful for defending *Paraceratherium* against predators, although most meat-eaters were not much bigger than today's wolf, so they posed little danger. It is likely that male *Paraceratheriums* had bigger tusks than females, so large tusks might have been seen as an attractive feature that helped to gain a mate. A modern rhinoceros uses its horns for similar purposes, as well as digging for groundwater and gently shoving young rhinos in the right direction.

Paraceratherium Facts

CLASS	Mammals
ORDER	Perissodactyls
SUPERFAMILY	Rhinocerotoids
SPECIES	*Paraceratherium bugtiense*
RANGE	Europe and Asia
TIME PERIOD	34–23 million years ago
SIZE	7.3–7.5 m (24–24.6 ft) long

No fossil has preserved *Paraceratherium*'s skin, but paleontologists usually imagine it was thick, wrinkly, and mostly hairless, like a modern rhinoceros's. In most climates, very large mammals have little need for hair since their own body heat keeps them warm enough.

Phorusrhacids

Often called terror birds, these meat-eating birds grew to 3 m (10 ft) tall.
Like today's ostrich, they were unable to use their small wings for flight but could run
extremely fast, at up to 48 km/h (30 miles per hour). They were among the largest
and fiercest predators in their habitats.

KELENKEN

The largest known terror bird, *Kelenken* had
small wings, but long, powerful legs. It had
three large, clawed toes (a smaller fourth toe
did not touch the ground) for pinning down
prey. The bird's skull was more than 70 cm
(28 in) long, including a hooked, sharp-edged
beak made of bone and covered by tough horn.

PHORUSRHACOS

Discovered in 1887, this bird (and its family)
was named after the ancient Greek words for
"wrinkle bearer," due to the wrinkled surface
of its jaws. Paleontologists determined that
Phorusrhacos and its family evolved from birds
that could fly, losing this ability as they grew
bigger and stronger—making them fast-
moving ground-based predators instead.

PARAPHYSORNIS

A bulkier, squatter bird than some
of its relatives, *Paraphysornis* may
have lain in wait for prey instead of
running in pursuit. Bony ridges above
its eyes helped to shade them from
the sun as it watched and waited.

ANDALGALORNIS

Around 1.4 m (4.6 ft) tall, *Andalgalornis* had a slimmer, more lightweight body and beak than most terror birds. Its narrow beak was suited to reaching between rocks for hiding prey. The bird probably could not hold on to large, struggling prey with its beak, preferring to bash small prey against the ground.

Phorusrhacid Facts

CLASS	Birds
CLADE	Australaves
ORDER	Cariamiformes
RANGE	North America and South America
TIME PERIOD	62 million to 18,000 years ago
SIZE	1–3 m (3.3–9.8 ft) long

TITANIS

This bird's long, strong neck was suited to making repeated stabbing movements, while its hooked beak could tear through flesh. *Titanis* probably preyed on mammals such as large rodents and deerlike plant-eaters known as proterotheriids.

PROCARIAMA

This terror bird's name means "before cariama," referring to the modern, meat-eating bird known as the crested cariama. The cariama, a South American bird, is the closest living relative of the terror birds, although it reaches only 90 cm (35 in) tall.

La Brea Tar Pits

For thousands of years, sticky oil called tar has seeped up through the ground in what is today Hancock Park in Los Angeles, USA. The tar trapped and slowly preserved animals. Around 11,500 years ago, many huge animals, known as megafauna, lived near the tar pits.

Megafauna animals are those heavier than a human. Mega plant-eaters had evolved to be large so they could reach more food, while mega meat-eaters had grown big to attack the plant-eaters. More meat-eaters than plant-eaters have been found in the tar pits because, when plant-eaters became stuck, predators came from far and wide, then also got stuck.

By 11,500 years ago, modern humans—having evolved from our ape ancestors around 300,000 years ago—were living near La Brea. Over the next few thousand years, humans wiped out most of the world's megafauna through overhunting.

COLUMBIAN MAMMOTH

A relative of modern elephants, this mammoth became extinct around 11,000 years ago due to human hunting and rising temperatures at the end of the last ice age (115,000–11,700 years ago). With their thick fur, mammoths were adapted to the ice age, when Earth was colder than today.

DIRE WOLF

A pack of dire wolves could kill prey much larger than themselves, including ground sloths, camels, and even mammoths. Over 2 m (6.6 ft) long, a dire wolf had a bigger jaw and stronger bite force than any modern wolf.

WOODWARD'S EAGLE

One of the largest eagles that ever lived, this bird of prey had a wingspan of over 3 m (9.8 ft). It seized mammals and reptiles with its sharp, curving claws, known as talons.

CAMELOPS

This camel was 3 m (9.8 ft) tall and weighed 1,000 kg (2,200 lb). Today, true camels live only in Asia and Africa, but they evolved in North America around 3 million years ago. It is not known for sure if *Camelops* had a hump for storing energy-holding fat like a modern camel.

SMILODON

Smilodon leaped on large prey, piercing with its sharp claws, then gave a bite to the neck or head with its canine teeth, which reached 28 cm (11 in) long. *Smilodon* was the size of a modern lion, but had bulkier bones and stronger muscles.

JEFFERSON'S GROUND SLOTH

Related to modern tree-dwelling sloths, this giant sloth—around 3 m (9.8 ft) long—lumbered across the ground in search of leaves. It used its long claws to reach high branches, then curled its flexible tongue around leaves.

Megalodon

Megalodon (meaning "big tooth" in ancient Greek) was probably the largest shark—and one of the largest fish—that ever lived. Since its fossils are incomplete, paleontologists disagree over this huge fish's exact size, but it may have reached 20.3 m (66.6 ft), at least 2 m (6.6 ft) longer than today's biggest fish, the whale shark.

KILLER FISH

The first fish evolved around 530 million years ago. Sharks were swimming in the oceans by about 420 million years ago. Unlike most fish, sharks have skeletons made of lightweight, bendy cartilage rather than bone. Along with today's great white shark, *Megalodon* was in the Lamniformes order of sharks, also known as mackerel sharks. Like its modern relative, *Megalodon* was an apex predator, so big and sharp-toothed that, as an adult, it had no predators.

At 18 cm (7 in) long, *Megalodon*'s teeth were the biggest of any known shark. They were sharp and jagged-edged, which helped them slice through bone. *Megalodon* had more than 250 teeth arranged in five rows. When a tooth in the front row fell out, the teeth in the rows behind moved forward to take its place. Due to the size of its massive jaws and jaw muscles, the force of *Megalodon*'s bite was up to ten times that of the great white shark.

Megalodon pursues *Eotaria*, an extinct species of fur seal. The shark could probably swim at up to 18 km/h (11 miles per hour) by beating its crescent-shaped tail.

FACING COMPETITION

Megalodon probably hunted alone. It usually fed on small whales, but it also ate fish, dolphins, seals, and sea turtles. The shark faced some competition from other large predators, now extinct, including macroraptorial sperm whales, which grew up to 17.5 m (57.4 ft) long, and shark-toothed dolphins, which reached 6 m (19.7 ft) long.

Eventually, *Megalodon* was driven to extinction by a series of changes. The first of these was the cooling of the oceans as Earth entered a period of colder weather. At the same time, many species of smaller whales died out. Surviving small whale species were faster swimmers and harder for *Megalodon* to catch. *Megalodon* also faced increasing competition from new shark species, such as the great white shark, which reaches 6.1 m (20 ft) long. The warmer oceans suited the great white, which was an excellent hunter of smaller, faster prey than its huge relative. All this was catastrophic for *Megalodon*.

Megalodon Facts

CLASS	Cartilaginous fish
ORDER	Lamniform sharks
FAMILY	Otodontids
SPECIES	*Otodus megalodon*
RANGE	All oceans
TIME PERIOD	23–3.6 million years ago
SIZE	14–20.3 m (45.9–66.6 ft)

Crocodylomorphs

Crocodylomorphs include modern crocodiles, alligators, caimans, and gharials, as well as many extinct crocodile-like reptiles that lived before, during, and after dinosaur times. Modern crocodylomorphs are the closest living relatives of birds, the two groups being the only survivors of the archosaur group of reptiles, which once included dinosaurs and pterosaurs.

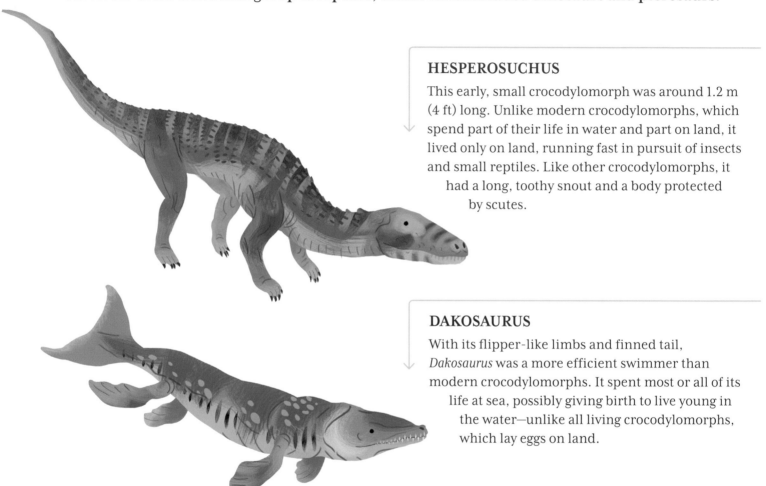

HESPEROSUCHUS

This early, small crocodylomorph was around 1.2 m (4 ft) long. Unlike modern crocodylomorphs, which spend part of their life in water and part on land, it lived only on land, running fast in pursuit of insects and small reptiles. Like other crocodylomorphs, it had a long, toothy snout and a body protected by scutes.

DAKOSAURUS

With its flipper-like limbs and finned tail, *Dakosaurus* was a more efficient swimmer than modern crocodylomorphs. It spent most or all of its life at sea, possibly giving birth to live young in the water—unlike all living crocodylomorphs, which lay eggs on land.

PURUSSAURUS

Possibly the largest crocodylomorph that ever lived, *Purussaurus* may have grown over 10.9 m (35.8 ft) long. Its eyes, nostrils, and ears were on the top of its head, suggesting that it lay almost submerged in water as it waited for prey—such as fish, turtles, and dolphins—to pass. It became extinct around 5 million years ago.

MEKOSUCHUS

Around 2 m (6.6 ft) long, *Mekosuchus* was found in Australia and islands in the South Pacific Ocean until around 3,000 years ago, when it was hunted to extinction by humans. It was the last surviving crocodylomorph that lived only on land.

MOURASUCHUS

Mourasuchus had a broader, flatter snout than its relatives, as well as a much weaker bite. It may have fed by sweeping its open mouth through lake water, gulping in whole shoals of small fish. It then tightened its throat muscles to force out water, but trapped its prey with its teeth.

Crocodylomorph Facts

CLASS	Reptiles
SUPERORDER	Archosaurs
CLADE	Pseudosuchians
RANGE	All continents
TIME PERIOD	235 million years ago to the present
SIZE	1–10.9 m (3.3–35.8 ft) long

GRYPOSUCHUS

Up to 10 m (33 ft) long, *Gryposuchus* was nearly 4 m (13 ft) longer than today's largest crocodilian, the saltwater crocodile. Between 16 and 5 million years ago, it lived in and around the swamps and rivers of South America.

Questions and Answers

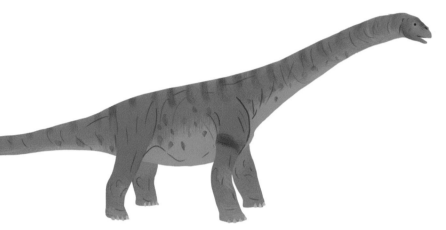

HOW BIG WAS THE LARGEST DINOSAUR?

The largest known dinosaur was *Argentinosaurus*, a plant-eater that lived in South America 96–92 million years ago. It weighed up to 75,000 kg (165,000 lb) and grew to 35 m (114.8 ft) long—the length of seven family cars.

WHICH DINOSAUR WAS SMALLEST?

Several feathered, meat-eating dinosaurs compete for the title of smallest, but one of the smallest ever found was *Anchiornis*, which lived in China 163–145 million years ago. It grew 34–40 cm (13–16 in) long and weighed 0.25 kg (0.55 lb).

WHICH DINOSAUR HAD THE BIGGEST TEETH?

The biggest teeth belonged to one of the fiercest meat-eaters that ever walked the Earth, *Tyrannosaurus*. This dinosaur's sharp teeth grew 30.5 cm (12 in) long.

HOW BIG WAS THE LARGEST INSECT THAT EVER LIVED?

One of the largest known insects was *Meganeura monyi*, a relative of modern dragonflies that lived around 300 million years ago. It measured more than 70 cm (28 in) from wingtip to wingtip.

HOW BIG WAS THE LARGEST SHARK THAT EVER LIVED?

The largest known shark, *Megalodon*, grew up to 20.3 m (66.6 ft) long. It may have weighed as much as 59,000 kg (130,000 lb).

WHICH ANIMALS WERE THE FIRST TO FLY?

The first flying animals were insects, around 325 million years ago. Next in the air were the flying reptiles known as pterosaurs (pictured), which flew 228 million years ago. Winged dinosaurs made it into the air 160 million years ago, as they slowly evolved into birds. The only other animals capable of true flight—the mammals known as bats—evolved 50 million years ago.

WHICH DINOSAUR COULD RUN FASTEST?

The meat-eating dinosaur *Gallimimus* was one of the fastest dinosaurs. Up to 6 m (19.7 ft) long, *Gallimimus* had long legs and a slim frame. It had an estimated running speed of up to 56 km/h (35 miles per hour).

WHICH DINOSAUR HAD THE LONGEST HORNS?

The longest horns belonged to the plant-eater *Triceratops* and its close relatives. The two brow horns of *Triceratops* were up to 1 m (3.3 ft) long.

WHICH DINOSAUR HAD THE LONGEST CLAWS?

The longest claws belonged to the plant-eater *Therizinosaurus*. Although the dinosaur probably did use its claws to defend itself, they were mainly useful for pulling leaves within reach. *Therizinosaurus*'s claws were 1 m (3.3 ft) long.

ARE ANY DINOSAURS ALIVE TODAY?

The dinosaurs were wiped out 66 million years ago after a giant space rock, called an asteroid, hit Earth. However, some dinosaurs had already developed beaks, feathers, and wings—and evolved into birds. Today, 10,000 species of birds are alive and well.

Glossary

amphibian
An animal that lays eggs in water and usually spends part of its life in water and part on land, such as a frog.

animal
A living thing that feeds on other living things, can sense and respond to the world around it, and can move at some point in its life.

ankylosaur
A thyreophoran dinosaur with defensive scutes and sometimes a tail club.

archosaur
An animal whose skull has a hole between the eye socket and nostril and another at the back of the lower jaw. Dinosaurs, pterosaurs, crocodiles, and birds are archosaurs.

asteroid
A rocky object that orbits the Sun in space.

bacterium (plural: bacteria)
A tiny living thing with one working part known as a cell.

bird
An animal that lays tough-shelled eggs and has a beak, wings, and feathers.

camouflage
The way the pattern and shape of an animal make it less visible in its habitat.

carnivore
An animal that eats other animals.

cerapod
A plant-eating dinosaur with a beak and ridged teeth.

ceratopsian
A cerapod dinosaur that often had horns and a neck frill.

class
A scientific group that includes animals with the same body plan, such as birds or mammals.

conifer
A tree that produces seeds inside cones and has needle-like or scale-like leaves that usually remain on the tree year-round.

continent
A large area of land, usually separated from other continents by ocean. Today, there are seven continents: Africa, Antarctica, Asia, Australia, Europe, North America, and South America.

crest
A growth of bone, scales, feathers, skin, or hair on the head or back of an animal.

Cretaceous Period
A period of Earth's history lasting from 145 to 66 million years ago.

cynodont
A member of a group of animals that includes mammals and their ancestors.

dinosaur
An extinct, land-living reptile that walked with its back legs held directly beneath its body.

dromaeosaur
A small theropod dinosaur with an extra-large claw on each back foot.

evolution
The process by which one species changes into another over millions of years, by passing on characteristics from one generation to the next.

extinction
When a species dies out completely.

family
A group of species that are closely related, so that they look and behave much alike. For example, lions and tigers are in the cat family.

feather
A light, fringed growth from the skin of birds and some dinosaurs. A feather has a tough central stem, with softer threads growing from either side. Feathers are made from keratin, which is also found in scales and hair.

fern
A flowerless plant that has feathery or leafy fronds and makes new plants by releasing tiny spores.

fish
A water-living animal, usually with fins and scales, that takes oxygen from the water using gills.

flowering plant
A plant that bears flowers and makes new plants by producing seeds contained within fruit.

fossil
The remains of an animal or plant that died long ago, preserved in rock.

gill
An organ that takes oxygen from water.

habitat
The natural home of an animal, plant, or other living thing.

herbivore
An animal that eats plants.

horn
A hard material, also called keratin, that is found in scales, feathers, beaks, claws, nails, and hair. Another meaning of "horn" is a pointed, bony growth on the head.

insect
An invertebrate with six legs and a three-part body.

invertebrate
An animal without a backbone, such as a squid, spider, or insect.

Jurassic Period
A period of Earth's history lasting from 201 to 145 million years ago.

keratin
A hard material that is found in scales, feathers, beaks, claws, nails, and hair.

mammal
An animal that grows hair at some point in its life and feeds its young on milk, such as a cat or human.

marine
Found in saltwater, in the ocean.

mate
A partner for making babies.

mineral
A solid, natural substance that forms in the ground or in water.

nodosaur
An ankylosaur with bumps and spikes on its skull, but no tail club.

nutrient
A substance needed by an animal's body for growth and health.

omnivore
An animal that eats both plants and animals.

order
A group of families that are closely related. For example, the cat and dog families are in the meat-eating Carnivora order.

oxygen
A gas that is in the air and is also part of water. Animals need oxygen to live.

pachycephalosaur
A cerapod dinosaur with a thick, often domed, skull.

paleontologist
A scientist who studies fossils.

predator
An animal that hunts other animals.

prey
An animal that is killed by another animal for food.

pseudosuchian
A member of a group of archosaurs that includes crocodiles and their relatives.

pterosaur
A flying reptile with wings made from skin stretched over a long fourth finger. A pterosaur was a relative of dinosaurs.

rain forest
A thick forest found in areas that are rainy throughout the year.

range
The area where an animal is found.

reptile
An animal that usually lays eggs on land and has skin covered in scales or scutes.

sauropodomorph
A long-necked, plant-eating dinosaur.

scale
A small, hard plate that grows from the skin of most fish and reptiles.

scute
A bony plate with a horny covering.

snout
The nose and mouth of an animal.

species
A group of living things that look very similar and can mate together.

spine
A long, pointed bone or body part. Another meaning of "spine" is an animal's backbone.

stegosaur
A thyreophoran dinosaur with rows of plates along its back and pairs of spikes at the end of its tail.

tetrapod
An animal with four limbs or with four-limbed ancestors, such as an amphibian, reptile, bird, or mammal.

theropod
A usually meat-eating dinosaur with hollow bones and, in many cases, three main toes.

thyreophoran
A plant-eating dinosaur with scutes for protection.

titanosaur
A huge sauropodomorph with a relatively small head.

Triassic Period
A period of Earth's history lasting from 252 to 201 million years ago.

vertebra (plural: vertebrae)
A small bone forming the backbone.

vertebrate
An animal with a backbone: a fish, amphibian, reptile, bird, or mammal.

wingspan
The width of a flying animal's outstretched wings, from wingtip to wingtip.

Pronunciation Guide

Agilisaurus Aj-i-lee-SAWR-us
Alaskacephale Ah-LASS-kuh-SEF-ah-lee
Albertonykus AL-buh-TON-i-kus
Allosaurus AL-oh-SAWR-us
Alvarezsaurus AL-ver-ez-SAWR-us
Anchiornis ANK-ee-OR-nis
Ankylosaurus Ang-KILE-uh-SAWR-us
Archaeopteryx ARK-ee-OPT-er-ix
Archelon ARK-ee-lon
Archosaur ARK-oh-SAWR
Argentinosaurus AH-gen-teen-uh-SAWR-us
Aristosuchus A-RISS-toe-SOOK-us
Baryonyx Bah-ree-ON-iks
Borealopelta BORE-ee-al-oh-PELT-uh
Brachiosaurus BRAK-ee-uh-SAWR-us
Cerapod SEH-ruh-POD
Ceratosaurus Seh-RAT-oh-SAWR-us
Citipati SIT-ee-PAT-ee
Coelophysis SEE-loh-FY-sis
Colepiocephale COL-ep-ee-oh-SEF-ah-lee
Compsognathus Comp-sog-NAY-thus
Cryolophosaurus CRY-oh-LOAF-oh-SAWR-us
Ctenochasma TEN-oh-KAZ-muh
Diabloceratops Dee-OB-low-SEH-ruh-tops
Dicraeosaurus Dye-KRAY-oh-SAWR-us
Dilophosaurus Dye-LOF-oh-SAWR-us
Dimetrodon Dye-MET-roh-don
Diplodocus Dip-loh-DOK-us
Dolichorhynchops DOL-ee-kor-IN-chops
Dubreuillosaurus Doo-BRY-oh-SAWR-us
Edmontosaurus Ed-MON-tuh-SAWR-us
Elasmosaurus Eh-LAZ-moh-SAWR-us
Eodromaeus Ee-oh-DROME-ay-us
Eoraptor EE-oh-RAP-tor
Eotyrannus Ee-oh-TIE-ran-us
Eudimorphodon You-dye-MAW-fuh-don
Euoplocephalus You-op-luh-SEF-uh-lus
Eustreptospondylus You-STREPT-oh-SPON-dee-lus
Gallimimus Gal-uh-MY-mus
Gargoyleosaurus Gahr-GOYL-ee-oh-SAWR-us
Giganotosaurus JIG-an-oh-tuh-SAWR-us
Giraffatitan Ji-RAF-uh-TIE-tan
Glacialisaurus GLAY-shall-ee-SAWR-us
Goyocephale GOY-oh-SEF-ah-lee
Graciliceratops GRAS-il-ee-SEH-ruh-tops
Halszkaraptor Hull-shka-RAP-tor

Herrerasaurus Huh-RARE-uh-SAWR-us
Hesperosuchus HES-per-ON-ik-us
Huayangosaurus Hwah-YAHNG-oh-SAWR-us
Hypsilophodon Hip-sih-LO-fuh-don
Ichthyosaur ICK-thee-oh-SAWR
Jiangxisaurus Gee-ANG-shee-SAWR-us
Kaatedocus KAHT-uh-DOH-kus
Kentrosaurus KEN-truh-SAWR-us
Linhenykus Lin-HAY-ni-kus
Lucianovenator LOO-chee-ah-NOV-en-ay-tor
Minotaurasaurus Min-uh-TAWR-uh-SAWR-us
Neuquensaurus New-KEN-SAWR-us
Omeisaurus OH-may-SAWR-us
Opisthocoelicaudia Op-IS-thoh-sil-ee-KAW-dee-uh
Oviraptor OH-vee-RAP-tor
Pachycephalosaurus Pak-ee-SEF-uh-lo-SAWR-us
Parasaurolophus Par-ah-SAWR-OL-uh-fus
Parvicursor Par-vee-KER-suh
Pentaceratops Pen-tah-SEH-ruh-tops
Plateosaurus PLAY-tee-uh-SAWR-us
Prenocephale PREE-noh-SEF-ah-lee
Protoceratops Pro-toe-SEH-ruh-tops
Pterodactylus TEH-roh-DAK-til-us
Pterosaur TEH-roh-sawr
Qiupanykus Chew-PAN-i-kus
Rhamphorhynchus RAM-for-INK-us
Saltasaurus Salt-uh-SAWR-us
Sauropodomorph SAWR-oh-POD-oh-MORF
Saurornithoides SAWR-or-nith-OY-dees
Scelidosaurus Skel-ee-doe-SAWR-us
Shuvuuia Shu-VOO-ee-ah
Spinosaurus SPINE-oh-SAWR-us
Stegoceras Steg-OSS-er-us
Stegosaurus STEG-uh-SAWR-us
Therizinosaurus THAIR-uh-zeen-uh-SAWR-us
Theropod Theh-ruh-POD
Thescelosaurus Theh-SEL-uh-SAWR-us
Thyreophoran THIGH-ree-oh-FOR-un
Torosaurus TORE-oh-SAWR-us
Triceratops Try-SEH-ruh-tops
Tsaagan SAR-gan
Tyrannosaurus Ty-RAN-oh-SAWR-us
Udanoceratops Oo-DARN-oh-SEH-ruh-tops
Velociraptor Veh-LOSS-ee-RAP-tor
Wiehenvenator VEE-en-VEN-ay-tor
Xuanhanosaurus Shwan-oh-SAWR-us

Index

Aetosauroides 35
Afrovenator 62
Agilisaurus 42
Alamosaurus 90
Alaskacephale 80
Albertonykus 86–87
Allosaurus 51
Almas 84
Alphadon 102
alvarezsaurids 86–87
Alvarezsaurus 87
ammonoids 12
amphibians 13, 14, 15, 20–21, 103, 109
Anchiornis 56–57, 122
Andesaurus 74
Angustinaripterus 43
ankylosaurs 9, 51, 72–73, 85
Ankylosaurus 9, 72
Anshunsaurus 28
Apatosaurus 54
Archaeopteryx 58
Archelon 77
archosaurs 9, 26
Arganaceras 25
Argentinosaurus 82–83, 122
Aristosuchus 69
Arthropleura 18–19
asteroid 4, 13, 66, 102–103, 123

Balanerpeton 20
Banji 105
Barosaurus 55
Baryonyx 70
birds 4, 9, 13, 40, 56–57, 58, 95, 103,
    108, 114–115, 117, 123
Bonatitan 91
Borealopelta 72
Brachiosaurus 51
Brontosaurus 55
Bunostegos 14, 24

Camposaurus 38
Carcharodontosaurus 79
cerapods 8, 40, 42, 66, 68, 69, 80–81,
    85, 88–89, 92–93, 95, 98–99, 100,
    101, 102, 103, 107

ceratopsians 8, 85, 95, 98–99, 100,
    101, 107
Ceratosaurus 50
Champsosaurus 95
Citipati 105
climate 26, 40, 66
coelophysids 38–39
Coelophysis 26, 38
Colepiocephale 66, 81
communication 7, 88–89, 105
Compsognathus 59
Concavenator 5
coprolites 10
Cretaceous Period 12, 66–107
crocodile-like reptiles 9, 35, 95,
    120, 121
Cryolophosaurus 41
Ctenochasma 59
cynodonts 32–33, 37

Dacentrurus 47
Dakotaraptor 94
Datousaurus 43
Diabloceratops 99
Dickinsonia 16
Dicraeosaurus 52–53
diets 6, 8, 9, 10
Dilophosaurus 48–49
Dimetrodon 15
dinosaur
    characteristics 6, 9
    early 26, 34–35, 36–37, 38–39
    groups 8–9
diplodocids 54–55
Diplodocus 8, 54
Djadokhta Formation 84–85
Dolichorhynchops 76
dromaeosaurids 84, 85, 94, 100–101
Dubreuillosaurus 6, 62

East Kirkton 20–21
Ediacaran Hills 16–17
Edmontosaurus 102
eggs 7, 14, 20, 21, 84, 104
Elasmosaurus 77
Eldeceeon 21

Eodromaeus 34
Eoraptor 36–37
Eotyrannus 68
Eryops 15
Eudimorphodon 30–31
Euoplocephalus 73
Eustreptospondylus 63
evolution 4, 12–13, 14, 16, 20, 26, 56
extinction 4, 12, 13, 26, 66, 102–103

feathers 7, 8
fish 13, 14, 15, 77, 118–119, 122
footprints 10
fossils 10–11, 12
Frenchman Formation 102–103

Gallimimus 67, 123
Gargoyleosaurus 51
Giganotosaurus 74–75
gills 13
Giraffatitan 60–61
Glacialisaurus 41
glyptodonts 109
Goyocephale 81
Graciliceratops 98
Guizhouichthyosaurus 28

hadrosaurs 88–89, 102
Halszkaraptor 84
Hell Creek Formation 94–95
herds 7, 10, 39, 89
Herrerasaurus 35
Hesperosaurus 40, 47
Huayangosaurus 43
humans 108, 116
Hylonomus 22–23
Hyperodapedon 35
Hypsilophodon 68

ichthyosaurs 28
iguanodonts 69
insects 19, 23, 50, 59, 122, 123
intelligence 61
invertebrates 13, 14, 16–17, 18–19, 21,
    23, 50, 59, 122, 123
Ischigualasto Formation 34–35, 36–37

Jiangxisaurus 104
Jurassic Period 12, 40–65

Kaatedocus 55
Keichousaurus 29
Kentrosaurus 47
Khaan 104
Kirktonecta 20
Kosmoceratops 99

La Brea tar pits 116–117
Lariosaurus 29
Liliensternus 27
Linhenykus 87
Loricatosaurus 46
Lucianovenator 6, 39

mammals 12, 26, 32, 33, 51, 95, 102,
    108, 109, 110–111, 112–113, 116–117
mammoths 116
Mantellisaurus 69
Mapusaurus 83
marine reptiles 28–29, 66, 76–77
marsupials 110–111
Megalodon 118–119, 122
megalosaurs 62–63
Megalosaurus 8, 63
Meganeura 18, 19
Megapnosaurus 39
millipedes 18–19
Miragaia 46
monkeys 109
Morrison Formation 50–51
mosasaurs 76

Nanoparia 6, 24
Neovenator 69
Neuquensaurus 90
nodosaurids 51, 72, 73

Oksoko 7, 105
Omeisaurus 7, 42
Opisthocoelicaudia 4, 91
Oryctodromeus 92–93
Oviraptor 7, 104
oviraptorids 104–105

pachycephalosaurs 8, 66, 80–81, 103
Pachycephalosaurus 80
paleontologists 6, 10, 11
Pangea 26
Panoplosaurus 7, 73

Panphagia 34
Paraceratherium 112–113
Parasaurolophus 88–89
pareiasaurs 24–25
Pareiasaurus 25
Parvicursor 86
Pelecanimimus 5
Pentaceratops 98
Pinacosaurus 85
Placodus 29
plants 26, 40, 66
Plateosaurus 27
plesiosaurs 76, 77
poop 10
Prenocephale 80
Probainognathus 37
Procompsognathus 38
Protoceratops 98, 100, 101
Psephochelys 29
pseudosuchians 9, 35, 120–121
Pterodactylus 59
pterosaurs 9, 26, 30–31, 43, 58, 59, 69

Qiupanykus 87

reptile
    characteristics 4, 6, 12
    early 22–23, 24–25, 35
    evolution 12, 14, 20, 21, 26, 28
Rhamphorhynchus 58
Rocasaurus 91

saltasaurids 90–91
Saltasaurus 90
sauropodomorphs 8, 27, 36, 40, 41,
    42, 43, 51, 52–53, 54–55, 60–61, 74,
    82–83, 90–91
Saurornithoides 85
scales 7, 8, 44
Scelidosaurus 44–45
scutes 7, 9, 44
Scutosaurus 24
Segisaurus 39
sharks 77, 118–119, 122
Shaximao Formation 43–43
Shuvuuia 86
Sillosuchus 35
Silvanerpeton 21
Silvisaraurus 72
skulls 9, 22, 25, 30, 36, 62, 80
snakes 111
Solnhofen Limestone 58–59

species 4, 8
Sphaerotholus 103
spiders 21
Spinosaurus 78–79
Squalicorax 77
Stegoceras 81
stegosaurs 9, 40, 43, 46–47
Stegosaurus 9, 46
Struthiomimus 94
suborders 8–9
Supersaurus 54
swimming reptiles 9, 28–29, 35, 66,
    76–77, 120–121

Tarbosaurus 67
terror birds 114–115
Tethys Ocean 28–29
Therizinosaurus 96–97, 123
theropods 8, 34, 36, 38–39, 40, 41, 43,
    48–49, 50, 51, 56–57, 58, 59, 62–63,
    64–65, 67, 68, 69, 70–71, 74–75,
    78–79, 83, 84, 85, 86–87, 94, 96–97,
    100–101, 104–105, 106–107
Thescelosaurus 103
thyreophorans 9, 40, 43, 44–45, 46–47,
    51, 72–73, 85
Torosaurus 95
Torvosaurus 62
Triassic Period 12, 26–39
Triceratops 8, 99, 107, 123
troodontids 84, 85
Tsaagan 85
turtles 77
Tylosaurus 76
tyrannosaurs 67, 106–107
Tyrannosaurus 106–107, 122

Udanoceratops 85

Velociraptor 100–101

Wessex Formation 68–69
Western Interior Seaway 76–77
Westlothiana 21
Wiehenvenator 63
Wightia 69

Xuanhanosaurus 43

Yi 64–65

Zanabazar 67